A GIRL'S GUIDE TO CHICAGO

KELLY RUSSELL

CONTENTS

To every girl, you are never too old or too young to follow your dreams.

To my Dad, Mom, and my little brother David, thank you for everything. We will always be the original four, and I love you all so much. To my amazing, loving, and wonderful husband for always supporting my dreams. You are my best friend and I love you with all my heart. And, to my Nanny, the original city girl who I know is always with me.

Also, to Jamie, thank you for helping me bring my book to life.

ISBN: (paperback) 978-1-7321182-0-1

ISBN: (eBook) 978-1-7321182-1-8

Cover design and Illustration: Kristina Vukmirovic

Book editor: Jamie Ward

Interior design: Kristen Forbes

INTRODUCTION

To My Dearest Readers,

I wrote this book, "A Girl's Guide to Chicago," because I wanted to share my dream and experiences of living in Chicago. Although some of the names have been changed and events have been slightly adjusted, these experiences I had are all true. Moving to a new country, a new city, or anywhere unfamiliar can be intimidating and uneasy. Always be proud of overcoming your fears to experience life and your own adventures.

Maybe, like me, your dream is moving to Chicago.

At the back of the book, there is a checklist of each place and location I experienced during my first year in the city. Whether you are new to Chicago, a native, or planning to visit, you can use the checklist to help you explore the city to create your own memories.

Good luck with your own adventure, and I hope you enjoy Chicago!

Love,
Kelly

PROLOGUE

I t's a chilly evening in mid-November, and my Mum has made shepherd's pie for dinner. It's one of her favorite comfort foods to make when it's cold outside. I am not a huge fan, so I'm picking apart my dinner by moving around the carrots with my fork. I notice that everyone is fairly quiet at the kitchen table this evening. My parents have not once asked me about my day or what I did at primary school. I look over at my two-year-old brother who is currently shoveling his meat and potatoes as fast as he can into his mouth.

"David, darling." Mum gently touches his arm. "Please slow down, you are going to hurt your tummy."

David ignores her and keeps on eating. I shake my head and continue to play with my carrots. I have never seen a kid eat so much, and although my brother is cute, he is a chubby little guy.

"Kelly, David, we actually have something that we want to talk to you both about." Dad takes a moment to clear his throat. I immediately stop playing with my food, put down my fork, and look up across the table at him. "What's wrong?"

"Don't worry, it isn't anything bad, but this is something that your Mum and I have seriously discussed and talked over for the last few weeks." My Dad pauses for a moment to make sure he had the right words before he continues. "I've been offered a new job. However, the job is not here in England. It's in the United States. We feel that it's a wonderful opportunity for our family. It's something new and very exciting, and not everyone gets an opportunity like this. So, we have decided that I should take the job, and we will be moving to the United States right before Christmas. I know this is quite a big and sudden move for all of us."

I look over at David. He is still working on his plate of food. His face is covered with potatoes. He does not really understand what all this means, and he shouldn't. He is way too little. "Elly." He cannot quite say Kelly yet. I look back at my parents and shake my head. Little boys are so disgusting.

I pick up my fork and again start playing with my food. "What about Nanny? Can she come too?"

"No Boots, I'm sorry." That's Dad's nickname for me ever since I can remember. "She can't come live with us, but she will be over as much as she can to visit. As of right now, my contract in the United States is only for about a year. So, at that time, we have the option to come back home to England."

"So, where are we moving to?"

"Illinois is the state and the city is called Chicago. Have you heard of it?"

"I think so. But, I've heard about New York City more in school."

"Well, Chicago is also a big city but not as big as New York City."

I nod my head in response. I like cities. I love exploring London with my Nanny. My Grandmother takes me all over London whenever we go to stay with her. She has lived in London all her life, and she knows all the fun places to take us.

"How are you feeling darling? I know it's a lot to take in."

"Hmmm, I don't know Mum. I think I'm okay. I guess. I'm not mad or anything. I don't know much about the United States, but I know it's very big and a cool place. Some of the kids at school tell us about their holidays there. It's where all the movies are made."

"Well Boots, that's in California, which is not close to Illinois, but I'm sure we can visit while we are there. But speaking of movies, we have a movie we thought we could watch after dinner, as a family. It's all about Chicago."

My parents were right. It is about a high school girl who reluctantly agrees to babysit three kids after she has been stood up by her boyfriend on their anniversary. She gets a call from a friend, who is in trouble in the city, and off she goes to the rescue, dragging the kids with her. On the way to Chicago, the car breaks down, beginning a domino effect of troubles throughout the city.

I am seven-and-a-half-years old. Luckily, I am smart enough to know that *Adventures in Babysitting* is just a movie. I laugh to myself, because it's probably not the best movie to get us all excited and introduce us to living in Chicago. It was definitely a dangerous adventure for those kids.

"Are you okay? Are you worried at all? I'm sure Chicago isn't really like that."

"Mum. I know it's just a movie."

"Okay. We didn't realize the movie would be kind of scary, and I know we have given you a lot of information tonight. You can always talk to us if you have any questions."

"I'm not worried at all, and I actually really liked the movie." I give both my parents a huge hug and tell them I am getting ready for bed.

I didn't want my parents to worry. Honestly, I wasn't worried. At only seven years old, I obviously didn't understand all that's involved in moving, especially to another country. Maybe I should be a little nervous about moving but I wasn't. I am honestly really excited about our big adventure all the way across the ocean.

Six weeks later, we are walking through the terminal at Heathrow Airport. David is screaming at the top of his lungs. "I hate America! I hate America!" He is crying hysterically and trying to hold onto Nanny for dear life.

"David, Nanny has to go, but we will see her again soon." Dad is trying his hardest to loosen my brother's grip on my Grandmother.

My parents look so embarrassed, but I chuckle and smile at my brother. You really can't take him anywhere. If he is not eating, he is usually throwing a fit. I also hug my Grandmother as tightly as I can because I will miss her so much. She is one of my favorite people in the world. But I am definitely not going to start a scene as my brother likes to do.

We are now at our gate and waiting. David is still crying. A pilot walks by on his way to board a plane and notices my brother crying. He stops directly in front of him, simply hands him a set of airplane wings, nods, smiles at my parents and walks away. My brother mumbles a thank you between his snotty tears, immediately stops crying, and starts playing with his new toy. Oh, thank goodness, he has finally stopped!

I look around the gate. Many questions are racing through my mind. There are so many people waiting to board this plane. Do all these people live in Chicago? I wonder if anyone else is moving just like us? Maybe they are just going to celebrate Christmas with an American family? I wonder how different Christmas is over in the United States? I am so fascinated by it all. I cannot believe we are actually moving to Chicago. A new place, new country, new home, new school, new friends, new everything. After my parents told us about our move, I began to look at maps and read books all about the United States. The country is so huge. So much bigger than England. I found it all exciting but also overwhelming.

The plane ride is extremely long, and once we get to O'Hare airport, the plane doors are frozen, so they have to de-ice the plane. Since, they cannot get the doors open to let us out, we have to sit on the plane and wait for another hour. It is December 21st. We have been told that Chicago is a lot colder than London, but a frozen plane? How crazy is that! It feels like an eternity when we are finally able to get off the plane.

After we go through customs and pick up our luggage, we need to look for a man holding a piece of paper with our last name. He will take us to our temporary corporate apartment. We find him, and after about a thirty-minute drive, we get there only to find there is no bedding in our rooms. So, we wait. Someone will bring it to us.

At this point, it is the middle of the night in England, and we are all exhausted. My parents keep telling David and me how good we are and that we can go to bed soon. They look exhausted too. *Finally*, someone comes with everything we need. We make the beds and crawl in between the sheets. I fall asleep immediately. I don't even have time to think about the fact that I'm in a new city and in a new home.

The next morning, I awake to an unfamiliar environment. It takes a few moments to realize that we are in Chicago. I replay the day before in my head. It is four days before Christmas, and we have four suitcases filled with our belongings. Most of that being clothes. The rest of our stuff will be delivered in crates by boat several weeks later. Since we have almost nothing with us to celebrate our first Christmas in Chicago, my parents decide it will be fun to head downtown and go shopping for presents. I am excited to see what the city is all about.

We get off the "L" train and I see the signs for a street called State Street. We follow the crowd up the dirty subway stairs into the hustle and bustle of the city streets. I am completely in awe of where I am. I notice right away the snow piled up high along the sidewalks. Something we don't really see in England. Cabs are honking, holiday bells are ringing, and I see Christmas decorations everywhere I look. I hear voices of excited families walking together along the sidewalks. Holiday shoppers, arms overflowing with tons of shopping bags, are trying to navigate the crowds to get into the next store, hoping to find those last-minute holiday presents.

Dad stops us to take a second to figure out where we are going, then we continue to walk down the street. With eyes wide-open, everything is immense to this seven-year-old girl. Dad stops us from walking any further. In front of us, there are huge, beautifully decorated window displays. The sign above says *Marshall Field's*.

"I think we can find everything we are looking for in here." Dad grabs my hand. The three of us follow him into the department store.

We walk inside *Marshall Field's*. Oh wow! I cannot believe this store! It is so magical and enormous. I look up to see floor upon floor of everything you could ever imagine wanting to shop for. Decorations and holiday gifts are everywhere you look. I have never seen anything like it.

David and I hold on tightly to my parents' hands as we mix among the crowds of holiday shoppers. We buy some new "cool" American clothes, and my brother and I each pick out a special gift for Christmas. I choose a CD player and my first ever CD by Kylie Minogue. She is my favorite British pop star. Already, Chicago is so cool and I feel so grown up with my new CD player.

We spend the rest of the day walking around and exploring some of the city. We head from State Street over to Michigan Avenue.

"Boots, you will like Michigan Avenue. It is a famous street here in Chicago and it also has the nickname The Magnificent Mile. It's a mile-long street of stores, restaurants, and hotels."

I look up at Dad and smile. I am just like him when it comes to learning about things, especially new places. I love to learn everything I can about a place I visit.

The wind suddenly whips around us, and the cold is something like I have never experienced before. Dad explains that the cold wind is coming off Lake Michigan. We walk across the Michigan Avenue bridge, and I see gigantic chunks of ice floating throughout the Chicago River.

As we continue down Michigan Avenue, I watch a few women with fancy coats and boots hurry around us. They remind me of fancy ladies from the movies. I hold on tighter to my Dad's hand, not because I am afraid but because I am so excited. It is late afternoon and already starting to get dark, and the sparkly Christmas lights on the trees and buildings light up Michigan Avenue. We pass more storefront decorations and even a few Christmas trees. London is definitely not as decorated as this during the holidays.

I look up in wonder at all the buildings along Michigan Avenue. Who works in those tall buildings, and who lives in those gorgeous high-rise apartments? I have only been here a few hours, but I already love being in this city. Everything in Chicago is so much bigger and taller than the buildings I am used to seeing in London.

Also, everyone in Chicago just seems so much cooler, especially in the way they dress and in the way they speak.

I want to be just like them. Everything about Chicago is so different. I want to live in this city! Yep, I definitely want to live right here when I grow up.

ONE

TWENTY SOMETHING YEARS LATER...

I t is late morning and there is still a lot of fresh snow along the sides of the highway from the night before. I'm glad it has stopped snowing because I'm driving into the city to look at a few apartments. With a budget of only twelve hundred dollars per month, it has been difficult finding something I really like, but I am not giving up hope. My dream will one day become a reality. I know it will. And hopefully soon.

A few months ago, I told my parents that after the holidays I was moving to Chicago. Ever since we moved here from England, my parents have known my obsession with living in the city. They knew that this day would come.

Two years after we moved to the United States, my Dad got a permanent job in Chicago. His company helped us get our permanent green cards. My parents thought living in the suburbs would be a better place for us, so they built a beautiful home in which my brother and I would grow up. It really was the American dream. We were suburban kids, and it was great, however, a big part of me wanted to be the kid who lived in the city.

I left my job as a preschool teacher in Naperville. I was sad to leave the children in my class who I truly loved, but I knew it was time. I was ready to make the big move to Chicago. I had to take the chance and follow my dream.

A few weeks ago, my brother asked if he could move with me to the city. He doesn't love the city like I do, but he said moving with me would be something different for him, since he is also starting out a new career and looking for a job. I said yes. It's nice not having to worry about living with a roommate I don't know, and my brother and I are pretty close. So now, my next step is to find the right apartment for us and get a new job.

As my drive to the city gets closer, the Chicago skyline comes into view. The brilliant jet-black *Sears Tower* and the *John Hancock* stand tall, as if they are guards protecting the city. Then the sign: North Lake Shore Drive. As I look over at the skyline, I feel the goosebumps on my arms!

Even on a gray and cloudy day, the city is still so exciting. Maybe it's in my head, but I can feel the energy. I know when I finally move here I will never be bored. There is always something to see and do. I love the tall glistening buildings, the art-deco mixed with mid-century modern architecture and, of course, the beautiful lake. Even on a cold day like today, there are people running, biking, and walking along the lakefront path.

I am coming up to the curve on Lake Shore Drive. Lake Michigan is on my right. It looks like an ocean. During the summer months the water turns a bright, beautiful turquoise. It is gorgeous, and I love being by the water. I am a Pisces so, it's in my nature for me to feel better when I'm close to water.

I approach the curve on Lake Shore. I gaze to my left, and there stands my favorite vintage condominiums majestically overlooking the lake and beautiful Lincoln Park.

My dream to live close to Michigan Avenue is a little out of my budget right now, so I plan to find an apartment either in Lincoln Park or Lakeview. I absolutely love the historic homes that give these cozy neighborhoods their character and vintage charm. Both neighborhoods are fairly close to downtown, and I can easily get to my beloved Michigan Avenue.

I checked out the two apartments on my list. I could tell right away none of them were for me. It was exhausting yet exhilarating at the same time. But, it's okay. I know my dream is right around the corner.

When I arrived home a few hours later, my Mum was at the kitchen table. She had just poured herself a cuppa tea. I pulled out a chair across from her, sat down, and sighed.

"Hello love. How was the drive back? How did today go? Did you see any apartments you liked?"

"The drive was good. Just a little traffic on my way back. But, no, today was a little disappointing. I was so excited this morning to be in the city to see both places."

I shift in my chair and continue.

"The first apartment seemed so promising and it looked so nice online, however it backed up to the "L" train. The rumbling sound of the "L" through the city is such big part of Chicago. I love hearing the train, but it made the whole place shake, and I feel like I would get tired of that after a few months. The other one was not the same apartment they had shown online."

"I'm sorry darling. Would you like a cuppa tea with me? It seems pretty tough finding something right now. Maybe you could wait a few months. I'm sure you could get your old serving job back while you look."

"Sure Mum, I'll have some tea. But no, I don't want to do that. I just left my preschool. That was such a big decision to leave. I'm going to keep looking. I will find something soon, I'm sure. I have some money saved, so I still have some time. It's only been a few weeks."

During the past few weeks, I applied for quite a few teaching jobs, and now I wait to get called for interviews. The public schools won't start hiring for months, so I have also put in applications to a few private preschools in the city.

I'm quite good at computers, and I'm a fast learner, so I put in applications for receptionist and front desk positions, just to give me more options.

I see a call coming in on my phone. It is from a 312 number. I answer it quickly.

"Hello?"

"Hello, is this Kelly?"

"Yes, it is."

"Hi. We are looking for a receptionist for our digital marketing agency. I came across your resume, and I know it's kind of last minute, but would you be able to come in tomorrow and interview with us?"

"Actually, yes I can."

"Okay, that would be great. Let's say for . . . hmmm looking at my calendar . . . for eleven tomorrow. Does that work for you?"

"Yes, I can be there at eleven."

"Okay, great. I have your email here. I'm going to send you a confirmation with the time and our address, but we are located right on Michigan Avenue."

"Michigan Avenue? Wow! Yeah. Okay. Perfect."

"Okay, great. So. I will see you tomorrow and, oh yeah, ask for James. That's me."

"Okay, James. Thank you so much. See you tomorrow." I look over at Mum and give her a big smile.

"So, who was that darling?"

"Well, that was a call for an interview. One of the receptionist positions I applied for. They want me to come in tomorrow at eleven."

"Wow, that's great darling! Fingers crossed."

"I know! See Mum, I told you it will happen. The office is also on Michigan Avenue. So, how cool would that be!"

"That would be, and I hope tomorrow goes well for you."

The next morning, I am sitting across from James. He is asking me a few basic interview questions. You know the drill. Questions like: "Why would you be a good fit?" "What's your background?" "What are your computer skills?"

James is really nice and friendly. Our conversation is going well. I have a great vibe about this place and the job, and I really think I might actually be a good fit.

"So, Kelly, it has been great talking with you, and I feel like you could be a great addition to our team. However, let's go talk to my boss for a few minutes, because I'm sure he will have some questions for you."

"Sounds great!" I try to sound as cheery as I can as I follow him down the hallway to the next office.

"Hey Vin, this is Kelly. I'm interviewing her for the front desk position. Do you have any questions for her?"

I am standing right in the doorway and this Vin guy barely looks up from his computer. He is too busy with whatever he is doing. I instantly feel like I am bothering him. Finally, after what feels like an eternity, he looks up from his computer, and he gives James a look, as he grabs my resume from his hand. He is clearly not interested in interviewing me at all.

"Okay, so why do you want to work here, it says you are a teacher?"

I don't know why, but I suddenly feel really thrown off. This is obviously the last thing he wants to be doing right now. Why couldn't James have prepared him first that I was coming into his office?

Suddenly my mind is blank. I cannot think of what to say, so I just start talking about how the state doesn't really support teachers, and I'm not sure teaching is the right avenue for me anymore.

Oh my gosh! What! Who am I kidding? Where did all that come from? What am I talking about? I love teaching. But, I also really want this job, so I continue to say anything at this point to let him know that I do not want to be a teacher.

After my horrible interview with Vin and having no idea what I have just told him, I thank James and leave the office. I head to the Starbucks right below the building to call my Mum. She answers almost right away.

"How did your interview go, darling?"

"It went pretty well. I think. They told me I will find out if I got the job in the next few days."

"Oh, that sounds great darling. Fingers crossed."

Trying to forget about my interview with Vin, I hang up the phone, order my favorite Starbucks, a tall white chocolate mocha, no whip, and get into a cab that is waiting right outside.

"Union Station on Adams, please."

The cab driver quickly heads off. Just saying that gave me such a thrill. Maybe my interview didn't go as planned, but I still love being in this city!

It is late in the afternoon the following Friday, almost a week after my interview at the agency. I have been waiting for a call all week from James hoping to get the job. Since, it is almost five this obviously means I didn't get the job, and I should probably give up entirely on the position. Oh well. I have a few interviews next week and maybe it is for the best since my interaction with that Vin guy wasn't so good.

I grab my phone to text my friend that I hadn't heard anything, and it starts ringing in my hand with a call from a 312 number. My heart is racing, and I answer the phone.

"Hello."

"Hello, Kelly! It's James. Sorry for the late response. It's been a crazy week here. We didn't forget about you, and we hope you are still interested in the receptionist position because you got the job! It would be great if you are able to start on Monday, January 28th."

"Oh! Yes! Thank you so much! Thank you for calling, James. I cannot wait to start, see you then."

"Okay, great. I'll email you with a few details. Thank you, Kelly."

I hang up the phone, find Mum in the kitchen, and throw my arms around her to give her a huge hug.

"Mum! Oh my gosh! I got the job! The one on Michigan Avenue! I'm going to be a receptionist in the city!"

"I'm so proud of you darling. I knew you would get one."

"Thanks Mum." I am grinning from ear to ear. "Now, I have to keep looking for my apartment."

"Well, you can always stay here for a bit longer and commute with your Dad."

I knew that was an option, but I really didn't want to do that. My Dad has been commuting to Chicago from the suburbs for years. Although he works pretty close to Union Station, the commute is exhausting for him. Even if it is just for a few weeks, I really don't want to do that unless I really have to. I want to move into my new apartment in the city and start my job around the same time. I want my dream and the whole city experience all at once. I got the job, now I need to find the perfect apartment. So, that means I have less than two weeks to find an apartment and move.

"No. I think I will spend the next two weeks looking. I know my apartment is out there. I obviously just have to find it."

I meet up again with my apartment leasing agent, and we park right outside the apartment we are going to look at.

"Okay, we are going to have a look at this one."

I get out of the car and look up to where he is pointing. It is a pretty white three-flat house with a red door. The house is located on, what will be in the summertime, a pretty tree-lined street in Lakeview. It is in a great location, right on George Street and Sheffield Avenue.

I have a good feeling about it. I just know it is going to be the one the second we walk toward the building.

The leasing agency tells me that it is a traditional-style Chicago apartment and that sounds okay with me. The apartment is on the second floor. We walk inside, and the apartment is quite large and spacious, but it isn't updated at all. The kitchen is all white but definitely older. The apartment has a lot of character with crown molding and all the vintage charm that I love, including large bay windows in the front. There is a smaller bedroom in the front next to the living room and another just off the kitchen. The floors are creaky and uneven, but it is mostly clean. I know once I give it a good scrub and make it my own, it will be perfect. I am totally sold! I am so thrilled that it is in a neighborhood that I love and close to the train, so I can easily commute downtown to my new job.

"I'll take it. It's perfect. So, what do I have to do now?"

"Great." He looks relieved after all the showings we have had over the last few weeks. "I think it's a good choice for you. I don't think you will find anything better with your budget. We can start heading back to the leasing office and get your paperwork started."

I nod in agreement and spend a few more minutes walking

around, checking out my new apartment. I honestly do not want to leave. I wish I could move in right now.

We get into his car and drive back toward the leasing agency on Broadway, and I sign the paperwork and lease agreement on my very first city apartment. About an hour later, I walk out of the office into the cold, dark winter days of January with a big smile on my face. I cannot believe this is happening. Between job searching and apartment hunting these last few weeks, I have found an apartment that I love. I am officially moving to Chicago in less than two weeks!

TWO

It is the end of January and very cold, but it is a bright, beautiful day in Chicago. I am really nervous, but I could also squeal with excitement as we drive along Lake Shore Drive. Today is the day! I am doing it! I am following my dream. One that I have had since I was a little seven-year-old girl. I am finally moving to the city! I gaze out the window and see the Lake and the lovely vintage apartments along the lakefront, and I think to myself that this view will never get old. After years of wanting to live here, it is actually happening. This city is going to be my new home.

My Dad, brother, and I pulled onto George Street with our rented U-Haul. My parents have been so generous about our move. Stored in the basement was a set of their older couches, an old kitchen table, boxes of kitchen plates, pans, and utensils. They said we could have it all. We packed up our bedroom furniture and, of course, all our clothes and personal items into suitcases and boxes. A few of mine and David's good friends are meeting us in the city to help us move and lift some of the bigger items. Later on, we plan to celebrate and go out to dinner.

We open the door to our new apartment and go inside. David right away starts yelling, "Okay, this room is mine!"

I follow him to see which room he is claiming. Of course, it is the bigger room with two closets. He is such a brat, but I am too excited to argue with him. I grab one of my boxes and head into my new room. The other bedroom is at the front of the apartment, right next to the living room. It looks a lot smaller than I remembered, and I instantly notice that it does not have a closet. I walk out of the room disheartened, and Dad asks me what's wrong.

"My room doesn't even have a closet!"

My brother hears me and walks out of his room. He points to the closet next to the front door in the living room. "Well, you can have that storage closet right there. It's really big."

"Geez, David, thanks a lot!"

"Okay, kids, let's not yell. This is supposed to be an exciting day for both of you. Kelly, you can get a rolling rack for your clothes if you need extra room."

I roll my eyes at my Dad, turn and walk away from both of them. My friends Heather and David just arrived and follow behind me. I will figure it out, I told myself. I will not let this ruin anything. But trust my brother for taking the good room!

I give my two friends a hug and let out a big sigh.

"What's going on?"

"Oh, just my brother is being a brat. He doesn't even wait two seconds before he takes the better room with two closets."

My friend David rolls his eyes.

"That doesn't seem fair," says Heather. "You found this apartment, put in all the work, and it's your dream. You should get to pick."

"Yep, I agree. Oh well, I will make it work in here."

We all turn and look around my tiny room. They both give me a look as if to ask what I can do, and I shrug my shoulders feeling agitated.

"Come on. Let's get this move over with so we can celebrate."

Dad has gone home. We take a much-needed break and decide it is time for dinner. My brother's friend suggests we all go to a place called *Osteria Via Stato* on State Street downtown. I'm still upset with David about the room situation, but it not his friend's fault, and it sounds like a fun Italian restaurant. We all take a few minutes to freshen up, change, and ride in separate cars downtown.

Osteria Via Stato is the perfect place to eat after spending the day moving boxes and lifting furniture. We are all seated, and one of the servers delivers to our table glasses of water and warm, crusty French bread with fresh garlic and oil for dipping. We polished off the first loaf just as the waiter comes to the table. He must have watched us devour it all and greets us with another loaf of bread. We are all starving, so we order our meals straightaway. After dinner, David decides to stay out with his friends. Heather, my friend David, and I are tired from the day. I am also stuffed from all the meatballs, calamari, and penne pasta that we shared. It is getting late, and they are ready to head back to the suburbs.

I give them each a giant hug goodbye. "You guys. I really, really appreciate you helping us today."

"You're welcome," Heather replied. "It was fun to see your new place. I can't wait to come up and spend the night."

"Please, anytime, Heather, and we'll have a fun girls night soon." I look over at David. "You are welcome too of course."

"Okay, we will see you soon then."

I wave goodbye and watch David and Heather as they walk toward their car. Okay, now what? I am standing outside the restaurant and wondering how I will get home. I really have to figure out public transportation at some point. But obviously not tonight. It is late and best to just take a cab home.

I raise out my hand to signal a cab. Several pass me by. It is a busy night on State Street, but finally one slows down toward the curb and stops. I hop in and give him my new address. I cannot believe it cost almost twenty dollars to get back to my apartment. I cannot afford to do this every time I want to go somewhere. Geez! Cabs are really expensive!

I stay up 'til the early morning hours and have unpacked almost everything. I just want to get it done, and I really hate living out of boxes. My brother strolls in around two in the morning and is so surprised that already our apartment is almost completely put together.

"Wow! Kelly, you have done a lot. It looks so nice in here."

"Yep, it does, you're welcome."

I am still a little upset with him and didn't feel like talking. I get up from the couch and head off to my bedroom.

"Good night!"

I mumble goodnight back to him and walk into my tiny, no closet of a room. Okay, who was I trying to kid? I am living in a den!

The next morning, we sort out the last of the boxes. I know that tomorrow is Monday, and I have to take the 'L' downtown to my new job. David and I agree to take a practice run before I take the train by myself. We walk to the station, pay for a week-long pass, and walk up the stairs to the side of the platform that says The Loop. Okay, that seems easy enough.

We ride the train southbound, all the way downtown and around The Loop to the State and Lake stop. We get off and walk toward my new office. I feel so much better and much, much more confident knowing where I will be going in the morning.

"Your new office looks like it's in a really cool spot."

"Yeah, I think so too. I really appreciate you coming with me and helping me plan out my route. It definitely helps me feel less nervous about tomorrow."

"You're welcome. I don't mind at all. It's nice to get out and explore the city a bit."

I look at David with a big smile. "I totally agree. Come on. Let's go get some lunch."

We continue walking north up Michigan Avenue, and we end up at the *Grand Lux Cafe*. I have eaten here many times over the years, so it is easy and familiar. After our lunch, we walk off our meals and browse around the stores It is late January and getting dark and cold. And my feet! They're killing me!

I made the bad decision to wear my pointed-toe boots with heels that I always wear—not a good choice for walking around the city. What type of shoes do other girls wear to look cute and still be able to walk around? I am definitely not used to doing this much walking. Maybe I just have to get used to it? Yes, I decide this is the case and try to ignore the pain in my feet. I will just focus on enjoying the rest of the day, but all I really want to do is hop in a cab and head home.

So, I am wincing with every step in my pointed-toe boots, and I look over at David. He is happy as a clam–in his tennis shoes. Ugh, guys! It is so easy for them.

"David, do your feet hurt?"

"No. Why?"

"My feet are killing me! I don't think I can walk around much more."

He looks down at my boots and laughs. "Why are you wearing those heels?"

"They are not big heels, just kitten heels and these boots are usually fine. Just not when I'm doing all this walking."

"That's ridiculous. You need tennis shoes or something."

"I know, but they don't look as cute with my outfit.

"You are so silly, no one cares.

"Well, I do."

"Okay, well, it's getting cold anyway, let's head back to the train."

"Okay, good! Let's go"

Just when I feel like I cannot walk another step, we are on the train and headed home. This time we take the Red Line, then switch at the Fullerton station to get on the Brown Line, go one stop to the Diversey station, and we are home! It is so confusing, but I am just happy to be sitting down. City living is exhausting!

I wake up on Monday morning, and I am nervous. I am panicking a little, my body is moving a little too slow, and I feel a little light-headed.

"David?" He is still in bed. "Can you please come with me on the train again this morning? I don't think I remember where I'm going. I just feel so nervous to go on the train alone."

What has had happened to me? I was fine this weekend. Quit being so nervous, I tell myself. I know where to go. I am supposed to be this cool new city girl who can do anything.

I am being a huge pain, I know, but thankfully David is okay going with me. Maybe he is still feeling guilty about the bedroom?

I try to calm my nerves. I take slow breaths. I face the mirror and finish straightening my hair and perfecting my makeup. I decide on a black skirt and a blue blouse that goes nicely with my blonde hair. Professional but not over the top.

"Wow, you look nice," says David, as I make my grand exit from the bathroom. I respond with a weak smile.

"Kelly, you will be fine. Everyone is nervous on their first day. By the end of the week, this will all be easy for you."

"Thanks, I really hope so."

We do exactly the same thing we did yesterday. David is with me on the train all the way downtown and walks with me to the Starbuck below my office. I order a white mocha with no whip. I do love my morning coffee, but I also think drinking coffee is just what you do when you work in an office. At least, that is what people always did in the movies, and I just really want to fit in. I grab my coffee, and we head back outside.

"Okay, good luck! Let me know how it goes."

"Okay, thanks! I will! Thank you also for coming with me."

"Of course, I get it."

I give my brother a wave and walk through the doors of my building. My coffee held confidently in hand, I walk into the office. Already everyone is busy at work on their computers. A guy with tufts of bright red hair poking out of a torn-up baseball cap walks toward me and points to a desk.

"You must be the new receptionist. You can have a seat, and I'm sure James will be with you shortly."

"Okay, thank you." My voice is almost a whisper. I give him a smile and try not look nervous. I sit down in my chair at my new desk.

I look around at my new office. Big glass doors greet people at the front entrance that is just a few feet from my desk. The team is spread out behind me in a very large open layout. Most of the desks are all filled with my new co-workers who are busy tap, tap, tapping on their computers. There are no cubicles, only large desks grouped together by twos or threes. Each person has multiple monitors. The entire office is minimal, mostly black and white. The only color is the company's logo on the sign behind my desk. The conference room and at least four offices are at the back of the office.

The glass doors open, and three really pretty girls walk in and head into another big open room to my left. They are chatting with each other and do not notice me. I wonder what their jobs are here?

Everyone is dressed so casually in their jeans, t-shirts, and '80s-style knit sweaters. I look down at my black skirt, blue blouse, tights, and heels. I am beginning to feel very out of place. James did not mention anything in his email about a dress code. I tell myself it doesn't matter, and I want to dress to impress. Of course, a casual sweater and jeans would not have been an appropriate choice for my first day.

I poke around my desk to see if there are any clues as to what I was expected to do, but after a few minutes, James comes over.

"Hi, Kelly! Let me show you around the office, and then we can get started."

"Okay. Sounds good!"

I follow him around, and he introduces me to an office mostly full of hippie-type guys and one girl with frizzy, dirty blonde hair and big blue eyes. She seems really shy. James walks me past her desk, but she barely looks up at me.

I am feeling shy too. I often get this way when I don't know anyone. I hardly say a word during my introductions to everyone.

My coworkers seem nice and very welcoming. I feel happy and somewhat at ease now. I was nervous. I feared that the office would be full of mean girls. I know, I am probably strange. But that is what I really thought. I obviously watch way too many movies.

James spends about an hour explaining my duties to me. My main responsibilities are answering the phones, scheduling meetings, and setting up the conference room for meetings, and cleaning it up afterward. I am very nervous about answering the phone. I am a little overwhelmed. Everything about this position is all so new to me.

"You look really worried. Do you have any questions?"

"No. I'm just a little nervous. It just seems like there is a lot to remember."

"I get it. But you will be fine. I promise you will pick everything up really quickly. There is no pressure to learn everything today."

I sigh a little. "Okay. Yeah. You are right."

"Give yourself a break. It's your first day."

"Okay, I will. Thank you for your help, James."

"Of course. We are going to be a team." He looks down at his watch. "I have to get my day started and check on some clients. So, why don't you settle in and I will check on you in a bit."

"Okay, Sounds good."

James was right. I need to give myself a break. This is my first day at a new job with new responsibilities and in a different environment.

"Oh, Kelly. One more thing. Vin will come over around noon and take you out for lunch."

I nod my head, smile, and walk back to my desk. I think to myself, oh great! I cannot wait. I wonder how Vin will be this time?

It is one thirty. Vin hasn't come over yet, and a few of the guys and the "shy girl" are headed out to lunch.

"Hey, you want to come with us?" It is the guy in the torn-up baseball cap.

"I'm supposed to go to lunch with Vin."

A guy with a huge head of dark curls chimes in, "Oh, he probably forgot. He won't care if you come with us. We're just going across the street to the deli and get sandwiches. We will be back in a few minutes."

I am rather hungry, and I want to get to know my new co-workers. After all, Vin was busy the first time I met him, so he probably did forget, and this little group is so sweet to have invited me to lunch. I feel a little relieved he hasn't come over. I am not sure if my second encounter with Vin would be any better.

"Okay. I'll come with you guys."

"Okay great, let's go."

I grab my coat and follow along to the deli.

I am back at my desk, and just as I start to take a bite of my sandwich, Vin comes over to apologize for missing lunch.

"I'm so sorry. It's been a busy morning, but let's go over some things this afternoon. Just stop by my office when you've finished your lunch."

Vin seems a little nicer today. I eat my lunch quickly. I do not want to keep Vin waiting too long. As soon as I am done, I brush the crumbs off my skirt, grab my mirror out of my purse and check for any leftover food or in my teeth. I quickly add some lip gloss and head to Vin's office.

I tap on his door lightly. "Come in," he says. I enter his office and see his dark, long arms relaxing around his head. He leans back in his chair.

"Hey! How's the first day?"

"Good so far. Lots to learn but I hope to learn everything quickly."

"That's good. I'm not worried. I'm sure you will."

We spend the rest of the afternoon going over more of my duties. He asks me what other things I would be interested in doing around the office.

"How do you feel about managing our schedules and doing a few things to help support the team?"

"I can do whatever you need me to do to help."

"Good. Well let's wrap up for the day and tomorrow I won't forget to take you to lunch. I always like to get to know my new employees."

I shut down my computer and leave the office for the day. My first day was actually pretty good. It has been somewhat seamless, and I have to say that I really enjoy this whole agency thing. I am standing outside on the sidewalk of busy Michigan Avenue. I stand there, taking a second to remember which way to go. Hopefully, I can remember how to get back home.

THREE

It is Tuesday morning, and I walk into the office for my second day of work. I sit down at my desk and look around. Just like yesterday, most of the team is at their desks working. I wonder what time they get here in the mornings? I turn on my computer and enjoy a few sips of my coffee. I look up as a guy in a white shirt, tie, a vest, designer jeans, and dark, thick, perfect hair comes charging through the glass office doors carrying a black Prada work bag. He looks like he just came straight from a modeling shoot. He stops at my desk, takes off his sunglasses, and looks at me.

"Where is my latte and coffee cake? Each day, I would like my coffee and coffee cake on the edge of your desk, so when I walk into the office, I can just grab it."

I look shockingly up at the guy who is now staring right back at me. Who the heck is this guy? Did I miss something? Yesterday, when Vin told me I would be assisting the team, he did not mention anything about him. The guy in the vest and designer jeans continues.

"Head down to Starbucks and get me a latte and a coffee cake."

I am so appalled that I just nod my head, stand up, and walk out the front glass doors. I walk out onto Michigan Avenue and back into Starbucks. I give the order to the barista.

The Starbucks barista looks at me and starts chuckling. "Oh, honey! This order must be for Mark!"

"Who? Oh . . . yes. I guess so."

The barista gives me a big smile. "Honey, oh my gosh! Mark is really something else. Guess I will be seeing you a lot more often then. I'm Frank."

"Kelly. Nice to meet you."

"You too, honey. Don't you worry. I'll get you that latte ASAP." He hands me the coffee cake, and I walk to the end of the bar to wait for the latte.

A few minutes later, I am back in the office with the latte and coffee cake in hand.

"James," I whisper his name as quietly as I can.

"Where is the office of the guy who just walked in? I think his name is Mark?"

James looks up from his desk and points to an office with the door closed. He gives me a smirk. "Good luck."

I walk over to the office and lightly knocked on the door. A voice says, "Come in." I open the door. Mark is sitting behind a giant dark wood desk with a glass top. The whole office is designed to look like something out of *Mad Men*, complete with a bar cart. The entire office is dark. Dark gray walls and dark wood floors. The complete opposite of the rest of the office.

"You can just put my latte and coffee cake there." He points to the edge of his oversized desk.

"You must be the new receptionist." I nod and quietly respond "Yes." I turn around and walk out, pulling the door closed behind me.

As I turn back around, I bump right into Vin as he is walking toward his office. "Oh, I'm so sorry!" I almost knock his coffee out of his hand.

"That's okay. Good morning."

"Hmm Vin, can I ask you a quick question? Who is that guy in there?" I follow him into his office. "You didn't mention anything about him yesterday."

"Oh, that's Mark. He's my partner for the modeling agency in the room right next to your desk. We all share this space."

"Modeling agency?"

Yeah, I'm also part owner of a promotional modeling agency." He points behind me to the room where the three pretty girls walked into yesterday. "The girls over there hire models to help with promotional events for our marketing clients around the city."

"Oh, interesting. Well, I just had no idea who he was. He came charging in and asked me to run out to Starbucks to get his morning order."

"Sorry, about that. He's from New York City, and he thinks that's the way it goes around here. Very *Devil Wears Prada* if you have ever seen that movie." I smile back at Vin. Of course, I know that movie, but I am more surprised that he knows that movie.

"I think he has the idea that your job is to personally assist him, even though I have told him that is not necessarily the case. He tried that a lot with our last receptionist."

"It's okay. I just don't want to pay for his Starbucks order every day."

"Oh. No. Of course not. Take some money out of petty cash. It's in your desk. I will talk to him about you getting his Starbucks. We can figure out together what you can and can't assist him with."

"Okay. Thanks. I just don't want to cause a huge or awkward problem."

"No problem." He sits down at his desk and opens his laptop.

The rest of the day is pretty much normal. I am just trying to learn and remember everything I am asked to do. After each meeting, I head to the conference room to clean up and set up for the next. I try to be as confident as I can whenever I answer the phone. It is my least favorite part of the job so far. I think I sound so stupid, and I do not always know what to say.

Today seems like a busy day. Everyone is buzzing around the office from meeting to meeting. I love this agency life, although it's so different from what I'm used to, it's exciting.

Mark comes over to my desk late morning. I look up at him, ready for whatever he is going to ask me to do next.

"Hey. Kelly, right?"

"That's me. Can I get something for you?"

"No. No. I'm sorry for this morning. I think we got off to a wrong start. I'm Mark." He puts out his hand. I stand up from my desk, so I can better shake his hand.

"Nice to officially meet you, Mark," I reply, sounding as professional as I can.

"If I'm running late, would you mind getting my Starbucks in the mornings? I'll give you my card when I come in. You'll know what to get. A grande latte and a piece of coffee cake."

"Okay. I can do that. No problem."

"Thanks, Kell. That would be so helpful."

Vin must have talked to him. I was so grateful for that. Maybe Vin wasn't so bad after all?

Just before lunch, Vin introduces me to the girls from the modeling agency. Amy, Natalie, and Kourtney. Amy has long brown hair. She is cute and sweet, and she has a causal style like mine. Kourtney is tall. She has light brown skin, silky brown hair, and a perfect body to match. I notice her style is amazing and her clothes fit her perfectly. Natalie is short and somewhat boxy with long hair down to her waist. She keeps her style and makeup very simple. She is naturally pretty.

These girls are really nice. Kourtney and Amy ask me a few questions to get to know me. As I am responding, I notice that Natalie is not listening. She is flirting with Vin, and he doesn't seem to mind. Maybe they have a thing? I look back to Amy and Kourtney. They each give me a look that expresses exactly what I am thinking.

"So. Kelly. We should go out for drinks next week or something after work?"

"I would love that. Sounds fun."

"Okay. We will figure out which day works for all of us and let you know," says Kourtney, but she is still watching Natalie.

"Great. I'm pretty much open. Just still getting settled. Anyway, it was nice to meet you all." I give one last look at Natalie who continues to chat away with Vin. I head back to my desk.

Vin comes to my desk around lunchtime and asks me if I want to get some lunch.

"There's a really great soup place at the Illinois Center across the street."

"Okay. Sounds good to me. Let me just grab my coat." I quickly put on my coat, grab my purse, and follow him out the front glass doors.

As Vin and I walk to Illinois Center, I really do not know what to talk about, and I am trying my hardest to just keep up with him. He is a fast walker. As we get to the corner of Michigan Avenue and Lake Street, the light quickly turns to the walk sign, and Vin immediately picks up his pace.

I must have looked ridiculous trying to keep up with him in my heels. I really need to get better city shoes. I think I will go to the store after work today. I especially need to get some better boots before it snows again. I will ask the girls in the office what they liked to wear. Obviously, I am thinking about my shoes way too much, and it is just ridiculous how much these heels are affecting my everyday life.

We walk into the Illinois Center and up the stairs to the soup place. Inside the Illinois Center, the line at the soup place is really long. It must be good, and we joke about the "The Soup Nazi" episode on *Seinfeld*. We wait about ten minutes to order but get our soup in a few minutes. We find an open table in the seating area and sit down. We open our soup containers and eat for a few minutes in silence.

"So. How do you like the city so far?"

"So far. So good. However, I haven't even been here a week. I moved into my apartment this past weekend right before I started this job. So, it's all very new and exciting."

"Wow. You are really new to the city. Where did you get an apartment?"

"In Lakeview. My brother is living with me."

"How's that going?"

"Okay. He took the better room. I have a tiny room with no closet."

"Hmm. Is that legal."

"I have no idea, but it's a huge pain to not have a closet." I switch the conversation to Vin because I am starting to feel angry again with my brother. I ask him about how he started the company and a few personal questions about him.

"Actually, I just moved with my girlfriend from Lakeview to an apartment in River North."

"Oh. Natalie?"

"What? Hmm no. I'm not dating her. We are just friends. I've been dating my girlfriend for a few years, but I'm not sure how interested I am now. I started feeling different about our relationship before we moved in. I thought living together would help, but it didn't. I feel myself pulling away from her."

I am a little shocked that he is so open with me. He is my boss. I barely know him. This situation must really be bothering him.

"Wow. That sounds like a tough situation. I'm sorry." I am careful not to overstep and say too much.

"So, can I ask you another question?"

"Yep, sure."

"The day I interviewed with you . . . you were really . . . umm . . . just, really . . . umm . . . not interested in interviewing me. It threw me off, and I'm sorry if I said anything weird about the whole teaching thing."

"That's not really a question. But, don't be sorry, you did great, and James really liked you. That's why you go the job."

"Umm, you're right, that wasn't a question. Okay, well, why did you act like that when I came in?"

"Was I mean? I'm sorry. Maybe just James threw me off. I wasn't expecting you to come in. I expected James to handle it all. I must have been too focused on something."

"Oh okay. I was just wondering anyways. You have been way nicer the last two days."

"Well, that's good. I'm not trying to be mean. I get engrossed in work sometimes."

We finish our lunch and hustle out in the cold and back to the office. "Hey, we should all go out sometime. Maybe plan a happy hour or something, you know, so you can get to know the team a little more."

"Yeah. That would be great. I'd like that. Thank you so much for lunch. The soup was really good."

"Good. Glad you liked it."

Moments later we are walking back through the glass doors, I am at my desk, and Vin heads back to his office. I am so pleased that lunch went well, and my boss is no longer acting the way he did during my interview. I am also glad I said something about my interview. I feel relieved about it because I have to work so closely with him every day.

My day ended around five, and I head toward the Brown Line. I decided to look for better boots this weekend. I am just too tired to do it this evening. It is already getting dark and I am feeling a little nervous, a little anxious to be walking alone to the train. It is only a few short blocks to the train and this was, after all, part of living in the city. I look around me, and the streets are busy with after-work traffic. Crowds of people are heading toward the train. I take a deep breath. I tell myself, I am okay.

My train ride to Diversey is about thirty minutes. I am headed down Sheffield and close to my street when I see a familiar face walking toward me. Suddenly, my heart starts to race, and I instantly feel anxious. It is Dylan.

Dylan is the guy that I had been dating. Yes, *had*. Over the last few months, I enjoyed coming up to the city to visit him. We spent a lot of time together hanging out, going to different bars and restaurants, and exploring the city's neighborhoods. He had also been great in helping me find a few neighborhoods where I would feel comfortable moving to. Dylan and I were introduced by a good friend of mine, and right away things were going well between us. We would see each other most weekends. I thought he was a great guy. The last few months had been fun, and I absolutely thought we were a couple.

However, literally days before I moved to the city, he stopped talking to me. I didn't want to think about it too much at the time, because I was eager to start my new life. I was little upset, broken-hearted, because I thought he was a great guy. What was also super strange is when I told him I signed my lease, he seemed excited. He told me that was perfect, because he found a place across the street from me. He said he was ready to move out of his sublet in Lincoln Park and into something nicer.

A few days later, he abruptly stopped talking to me. I was confused. Why would he want to move across the street, then days later stop returning my calls? I don't understand guys. The whole thing made no sense.

He sees me walking toward him, and I knew he was trying to figure out what do.

"Oh hi." He is now standing right in front of me, barely making eye contact. "How's the city so far? Can't believe you're here now."

"Yep, it's been amazing so far!" I am trying to sound cheery.

"That's great, maybe I'll see you around, get a coffee or something, good to see you."

He gives me a weak smile and continues walking. He is acting odd, and he clearly did not expect to run into me.

What was that! I wanted to yell out. I am so confused! What had happened? Who stops talking to someone just like that? Did he live in my neighborhood now? If he did, he must have just moved in too, but it seems way too quick. I thought about calling out his name, so I could ask him all these thoughts that were running through my head. I turn around to call out to him, but he is already too far away.

Now what? Should I text him? I look at my phone. I do not know what to say. I sigh and put my phone in my pocket, and I walk the rest of the way home feeling just so . . . blah. My mood has completely changed. I just could not understand what I did wrong. Just forget about him, I tell myself. This is an exciting time for you. Seriously, who cares about Dylan.

But I did care. I was really hurt. When I get home, I tell David about my extremely awkward encounter with Dylan.

"I'm so sorry. He's such an idiot. Seriously. Try not to let him affect all the good things you have going on right now."

My brother was right.

"Let's watch some episodes of *The Office*. That will help get your mind off things."

My brother had recently introduced me to the American version of *The Office*, and we were both completely hooked! I could not believe I hadn't watched it before. I, for one, could not get enough of Jim and Pam. I put on my comfy clothes and snuggled up on the couch under my blanket and wondered if I would I ever find someone like Jim?

FOUR

I think whenever you make a big life change, you kind of second guess it and ask yourself if you made the right choice. I love the city, and I love my new job, but I honestly have to say that I feel lonely.

This might sound silly since I am now living my dream, and I should really give my adjustment to life here some more time. It is only my second full week into my new life and I enjoy work and my new coworkers are great and have been so welcoming.

But apart from that and hanging out with my brother, I don't have much to do. I am not used to the emptiness of it all.

As much as I want to, and as much as I am trying, I am not confident about walking around the city by myself. I want to do more alone and to see and explore everything, but I am holding myself back.

Numerous times after work, I wanted to walk down Michigan Avenue and browse around some of the stores. But, I become almost paralyzed with fear at the thought of taking the train home too late and walking alone to my apartment. I am so bummed. Here I am! In Chicago! This is my dream. I should be experiencing everything in this city, especially after having this dream for so long.

It's Thursday of my second week of work and living in Chicago. I head home to make dinner and watch my newest obsession, *The Office*. Another somewhat lonely night. I guess staying home is okay, I mean, I really didn't need to go out anyway. I was hoping the girls in the office would ask me to go out and have drinks with them, but nothing has been planned. I should have asked them what they were up to for Friday night or the weekend, but I didn't. I was too shy to ask. So, what's the worse they'd say? That they already had plans? But I just couldn't bring myself to do it.

David is right, I do have a lot of good things going for me, and I should give myself more time to get settled and to adjust. I know I am a bit of a baby about it and impatient about making friends. However, I *do* know why I am feeling this way. I must be honest with myself about the real reason why I'm feeling weird about being alone and walking the city, especially at night. I need to help myself with this anxiety and get through it.

It's only been a few years since my traumatic event. I knew these feelings could come back once I moved. My fears and anxiety will probably come back over and over throughout my life.

What happened to me was so frightening, and it paralyzed me with fear for a very long time. I still have issues with it, and it has affected my confidence and exacerbated any feelings I had of being alone.

A few years ago, one evening after work I was going to my friend's house to meet up with a group of friends. I parked just outside the apartment building and walked toward the front door, just like I always did. I heard a voice call out to me from behind. I thought it was one of my guy friends, so I turned around to see a man dressed in all black, wearing a ski mask. Within seconds, he grabs me, puts a gun to my head, and grabs all of my belongings. I froze, paralyzed with fear, and waited for what he would do next. Luckily, just then, a car drove by, and its headlights lit us up. He hit me on the head with his gun and ran off.

I was stunned and terrified by what just happened, but I was alive! I ran up to my friend's house for help.

This happened close to where I lived, where I grew up, in my safe and cozy suburb. Yep, in the suburbs! This proves that bad things can happen anywhere. I still have issues with it, and the move to the city has brought out all my feelings of anxiety. I try to feel safe while I figure out how to live safely in the city.

I try hard to overcome my fear of walking alone. I need to just get out and do everything I want to do in the city. I want to get out of my apartment, go for a walk on a Saturday morning, grab a coffee, and explore my neighborhood. But, I just can't do it alone. Not yet anyway.

I feel stupid sometimes, and maybe there are some who think it is strange that I asked my brother to ride the train with me on my first day to work. It is hard for me to be out of my comfort zone. I'm determined, however, to get better at it and do everything I want to do. I will get over this little 'hiccup' and start to enjoy my life in the city.

The next day, Friday morning, I am getting ready for work, and David tells me he is heading home for the weekend.

"You should come with me. I can wait for you to you get off work today."

I pause by the bathroom door thinking about my options for this weekend. It's either hang out here alone or go home and see my parents.

"Okay. If you don't mind waiting. I can probably be at Union Station by five-thirty."

"Yeah I don't mind. I know Mum and Dad will be happy to have you home for the weekend."

We meet at Union Station on Friday after work and board the BNSF for the suburbs. I'm really looking forward to hanging out with Mum and Dad. My hometown isn't too far away, but when you live in the city and don't have a car, it can be a total pain to get home. Dad picks us up from train, and he's really happy to see us.

"Hi Dad!" I throw my arms around him as soon as I see him.

"Hi Boots! How was your few weeks of work?"

"It's really good. I really like it."

"Good to hear. I thought we could pick up Chinese for dinner before we head home. I know Mum is so excited to see you both."

"That sounds great. I'm starving."

We phone in our order while in the car and pick it up on the way home. As I walk into my parents' house, I get that familiar feeling of home. It's wonderful. I instantly feel like I'm going to cry. I hug Mum so tightly and tell her how much I missed her.

"I missed you too, darling. Is everything okay? What's wrong?"

At that moment, I feel like I could just move back home and forget all about my dream. I push back my tears and tell her how much I love my job and my apartment, but that I'm having a tough time going out on my own, especially once it becomes dark outside.

"Oh, sweetie. I'm so sorry. What can we do to help you feel better? Let me get some plates, and we can all sit down to eat and talk about it."

We all sit down to eat our Chinese food and all my feelings come out flooding out. David tells me that he will always come meet me or walk with me whenever I'm feeling nervous. It's really sweet of him. It really comforts me to know that my family is completely supportive and understanding of my fears and feelings.

After dinner, I definitely don't feel as crazy as I was earlier. Talking with my family has helped, and I no longer feel like I should pack up and move back home. I need to give my life in the city a chance. So, I have come up with a plan to make sure I have twenty dollars in the pocket of my purse at all times, so wherever I am in the city, if I'm feeling nervous, I can get into a cab and go home.

Saturday morning rolls around, we have our morning coffee, and Mum and I decide to head out to Target and Kohls, our normal suburban go-to on the weekends. It's a good feeling to be out and doing something familiar. My anxiety is gone, and I'm feeling so much better.

That night, I borrow Dad's car and head out to a bar called *Features* in Downtown Naperville. I am meeting up with my good friends. I park the car, and I walk into a somewhat crowded bar and spot those familiar faces. Excited to see them, I smile as they wave me over. I am feeling nostalgic. Maybe I made the wrong choice moving to Chicago? I try to push those feelings aside. I'm determined to enjoy a night out.

"How's the city and your new job?"

"My job is great, but I'm having trouble being alone, being out and about walking around by myself."

"Oh no," says Heather and comforts me by rubbing my arm. "Well, whenever you are feeling down, you can call me. You will get through this, you did before."

"I really hope so. It's a terrible feeling to be this nervous all the time. You should see me walking home from the train. I walk so fast down the middle of street, my neighbors must think I'm crazy."

We both look at each other and burst out laughing. It is a little silly to picture but, hey, it's good if you can laugh at yourself.

After spending Sunday morning with my parents, Dad drives us both back to the train station and take the 1:10 train back to the city. It's about a two-hour ride on the train on the weekends. When I get home, I want to relax, but I need to get my laundry done before I start the work week again.

Through the music on my headphones, I hear the conductor on the loudspeaker saying that Union Station is the last and final stop. We round the corner as the train heads towards the station. I look out the window and again I feel the excitement as I see all the familiar skyscrapers that I love so much.

David and I wait for passengers ahead of us to gather their things before we can get off. We get off the train and drag our heavy overnight bags to the Brown Line station a few blocks away. Although it's starting to get dark, I push away my nerves. I am feeling happy to be back here! Just like being at my parents' house, I feel like I'm going home. I'm determined to make my life here succeed. I'm going to start having fun, and I'm never going to regret moving to the city again.

FIVE

I spring out of bed as soon as my alarm goes off. It's Monday morning. I'm ready for work ten minutes before I need to leave for the train. Going home has helped me feel so much better. Deep down I knew that I made the right choice moving here. Sometimes you just need a different perspective. I'm determined to keep a positive attitude and get over my fears of being alone in the city. There is so much I want to see and do like exploring the different neighborhoods, eating at the newest restaurants, and learning about the history of this amazing city. I look forward to doing the little things, too, such as sipping coffee in a cozy neighborhood coffee shop or enjoying a fancy cocktail in a trendy bar. The support from my parents, my brother, and my friends really helps my confidence, and I'm grateful to them for that.

I walk into the office happy and ready to start a new week. "Hi guys! How was everyone's weekend?"

The guys are not used to having a girl in the office being bright-eyed and cheery on a Monday morning. They're barely awake and I get half-sleepy looks as they glance up at me from their computers.

"Morning Kell. How was your weekend?" James gives me a bright smile. At least someone else looks awake.

"It was good. I went home to the 'burbs for the weekend."

I am growing to like James. He is one of my favorites in the office. We have been chatting through Yahoo Messenger and I stop by his desk at least once a day to talk. He has a great sense of humor and always makes me laugh.

"What did you do?" I asked.

"Well, Friday night, my friends and I went to this place on Southport and Newport called *SoPo*."

"What's that? I have no idea where that is?"

It's in the Southport neighborhood, right next to Lakeview. *SoPo* is kind of a divey bar. I love it because they have five-dollar martinis all night, and they play the best music. Lots of pop mixed with '80s and hip-hop."

"Ooh! That sounds awesome!"

"You know what? We should go again this Friday. I think you will love it! My friends are going again, and you should meet them. They are really fun."

"This Friday? Okay! Yeah, for sure! That would be so fun! Okay, I will let you get to work, and I will chat with you later. I should get to my desk and start my day."

I walk over to my desk with an extra bounce in my step. Yay! I had city weekend plans, and it was only Monday. This is a great start to my week.

Mid-morning, I'm still in a good mood, so I decide to send Jillian, the "shy girl," an instant message. I've spoken to her a few times, and I'm interested in getting to know her better. She doesn't really talk to the other girls and, now that I think of it, she doesn't really talk to anyone. She mostly has her headphones on all day. So, before I can think too much about it, I tap out a message.

What are your plans for lunch today? I feel like we haven't really gotten to know each other. If you're not busy, do you want to go to lunch today?

The messenger bubble pops up right away, and she's typing back. That's a good sign. She responds, *Sure, 1 pm?*

Okay, sounds great, see you at lunch.

A little after one o'clock, Jillian walks over to my desk.

"Ready?"

"Yep. Just going to grab my coat."

"Do you like sushi? There is a good lunch sushi spot at the Illinois Center."

"I had lunch with Vin over at the Illinois Center. That must be a popular place to go. Is the sushi really good there?"

"Yep, it's really good. I promise. Going across the street is better than paying thirty dollars for lunch at a restaurant every day."

I nod in agreement. We take the elevator down and walk across to the Illinois Center. I decide that I can always get a California roll. You can't really mess those up.

The Illinois Center is super crowded again. The sushi place is a simple set up. You just pick up pre-made sushi in containers. They offer a variety, and it looks delicious. I still grab the California roll just to be safe.

We don't say much while in line to pay for our sushi. We look for a table and notice two girls getting up, so we rush over before anyone else grabs the table. As they get up, we set our sushi down on the table. We thank the girls for the table and sit down.

"So, how long have you worked at the agency?" I open my container and pull apart my chopsticks.

Jillian looks up at the ceiling, seeming to do the math in her head. "Oh. Only about six months."

"Oh really? I assumed longer for some reason. How do you like it?"

"It's good. I was tired of doing freelance stuff. It's tough not getting a regular paycheck each month."

"I can imagine, especially in the city."

"Yep."

I take a bite of my sushi, and it is really good. "So, how long have you been in Chicago for?"

"I moved here about two years ago after I graduated from Notre Dame."

"Oh wow! That's impressive."

"Thanks." She blushes a little and looks down. "I got a scholarship."

"That's great! Do you still freelance on stuff or work on any fun projects on the side?"

"Well, the coolest one is writing for a Chicago fashion and life-style blog called *Second City Style*."

"Oh my gosh! That is so cool!"

"Yeah, it is sometimes. I write about Chicago fashion and cover events in the city. So, it can be fun to go out, meet people, attend events for free, and get paid for it."

"For sure. That sounds really fun."

"Well, if you like that kind of stuff, you should come with me to an event sometime. I'll let you know when there's a good event coming up."

"I've always loved fashion, and I would love too. It sounds pretty amazing."

"Cool. I will definitely let you know. So, how're your first few weeks going? Where did you use to work before this?"

"It's going pretty well. I'm really enjoying what I'm doing. I was a preschool teacher, so this is totally a different world for me. However, I like my job so much that I think I'm going to put my teaching career on hold for the moment and focus on working at the agency."

"Well, that's great. I'm glad you like it so much."

"Yeah, me too."

We finish our sushi rolls and head back to the office. We chat a little more about what she does for the blog. It's really cool to hear about all the events she's attended and written about. I'm going to check out this blog when I get back to my desk. Since Jillian knows about the latest fashion trends, maybe she would know what shoes are cute and appropriate for the city. She might even want to help me out and go shopping with me.

I take off my coat and sit down at my desk. I get right up again to see if Vin is around. I don't see him at his desk. He must have gone to lunch. I quickly type in the name *Second City Style* into the Google search field. I click on the first website that comes up. The blog loads a few seconds later. It doesn't look that fancy. It's not as clean and chic like Vogue's website, but I can see that the blog not only covers events all over the city, but they also cover the latest in fashion trends as they relate to Chicago. This is seriously cool! I wonder how hard it is to get a blog up and going. I mean, I now work for a digital marketing agency. I'm sure one of the guys might want to help me.

After daydreaming for a while about the thought of having my own blog, I tell myself, okay, let's take a step back. One thing at a time. Let's figure out this whole city living thing first. However, I can't help but chat back and forth with Jillian a few times throughout the afternoon asking questions about the events she has gone to. I look at my computer, and I can't believe it's almost five o'clock. The first day of the week has been great. As I leave the office that evening, I don't even feel nervous walking down Lake Street toward the train.

The week continues to fly by, and before I know it, it's Friday. James and I made plans to go home, freshen up and change, and to meet up at *SoPo* around seven. I am looking forward to going out. I haven't been out in the city since I moved here, and I especially have not gone to a fun bar to go dancing.

I happen to be chatting with James at his desk about our plans for the evening when Vin walks over.

"Where are you two going?"

"We are going to *SoPo* at Southport and Newport in Lakeview." James looks over at me and grins.

"Oh. What's that? A restaurant?"

"No. It's just a dive bar with great dance music and good drink specials."

For a moment, Vin seems somewhat sad. Maybe it's because we didn't invite him. But do you really hang out with your boss outside of work? I don't think so. I don't think anyone from here does. It would be kind of weird.

"Well, have fun guys. Sounds like a cool place."

We both watch as Vin walks away.

"He's been kind of down the last few days."

I look back to James. "Yeah, I think he's going through some stuff. Do you think we should have invited him?"

"Nah. We've never hung out outside of work before. But maybe next time?"

"Yeah, maybe."

I glance toward Vin again, who is back at his computer. A part of me feels bad for him.

"Okay." I turn to face James again. "So, I'll see you later!"

"Yep! I'll text you when I'm in my cab."

At five o'clock on the dot, I close down my computer for the weekend and head out. I walk over and say goodbye to the girls at the modeling agency.

"Bye! Have fun! We will definitely do drinks next week."

"Sound good!" I wave to the three of them and push through the glass doors. As I'm walking down the hallway, I hear footsteps behind me. My heart begins to race. After being mugged, I really hate it when someone walks up from behind. I spin around, and it's Vin. My heart instantly returns to normal.

"Oh hi. So, I didn't ask you. What are you up to this weekend? Doing anything fun?"

"Not much. Just dinner tonight with the girlfriend and maybe the bars tomorrow night with the guys."

He didn't sound excited about any of this. I want to ask him what was wrong. But it just doesn't seem right or the right place. He's my boss after all, and we are not really friends.

"Well, that sounds fun. I hope things are better now."

"It's the same, but it's okay."

We walk out to Michigan Avenue and stop on the sidewalk.

"Okay. Well, have a good weekend. I'll see you on Monday!"

"Yeah, you too Kelly."

We part ways and walk in opposite directions.

I get off the train and walk as fast as I can to my apartment. It was already five-thirty. I need to shower and get ready for my first night out. I run up the stairs and into my second-floor apartment. David walks out of his room.

"Are you okay?" He's looking at me strangely.

"Yep! I'm great! Just wanted to get home quick and get ready for my night out."

"Oh. That's right. The way you ran up the stairs, I thought something was wrong. I forgot. Dancing with James." He changes his voice to sound dreamier.

"Umm. Do you think I like him or something? Because we are just friends. I'm absolutely pretty sure he's not into girls. He might be your type though?" I give him a playful look and smile. I totally wouldn't mind if my brother and my new friend started dating.

"Do you want to join us? You can definitely come. It will be fun!"

"Nah I can't. I'm getting up early to go home in the morning."

"Again?" I give him a sad face. "I was hoping that we could hang out together and do some city stuff."

"Sorry, I already made plans with friends at home."

I sigh and walk away. David has not spent one full weekend yet in the city. I need to sit down with him and see what was going on. We have only been here a few weeks so surely, he would want to be in the city on the weekends? Didn't he want to get to know the city like I do? I promise to talk to him this week. However, now isn't the time to start that long conversation. I have to jump in the shower and get ready for my night out.

I look around at my rolling rack of clothes. I really need to freshen up my wardrobe. Everything seems so outdated. I decide to wear a pair of black jeans, a black top, and my black boots. You can't go wrong with all black. Simple and casual.

I'm ready by six forty-five. I make a final outfit and makeup checks while I wait by my phone. At 7:04, James sends me a text me and says he's walking out to get a cab. I grab my coat, run into David's room, give him a hug goodbye, and I walk as fast as I can down the stairs.

Of course, it's dark out on my street, but a few people are walking about outside. Ahead, I can see cars at the top of my street at Sheffield. I hurry to reach the main road and look out for a cab. Luckily, one stops a few minutes later, and I get in. The driver asks, "Where to?" I pull up the directions on my phone. "3418 N. South-port." Two seconds later, I'm on my way.

There are a lot of people walking into the bar as I pull up.

Inside the bar is already busy. I pull out my license to show the guy at the door. He checks my I.D. and waves me in. I see James waving at me from the bar in front. His other hand is holding a red martini. As I walk over, the bartender puts another one down on the bar top.

"Here you go!" James yells over the loud music and passes me the drink.

"The first one's on me. I hope you like Cosmos."

"Thanks!" I yell back, grabbing the drink off the bar.

I take my first sip. You can tell it is cheap liquor. Too many of these and tomorrow will be a rough morning. Then again, who cares, tomorrow is Saturday. I didn't have any plans. It's time to have some fun and make the most of my night out.

We finish our first round of drinks rather quickly, and I order a second one for both of us. We get our drinks a few minutes later and head toward the side of the dance floor just as a Britney Spears remix came on.

"This is so fun!"

He nods in response. "Come on!" He grabs my free hand and we head toward where a bigger crowd is gathering on the dance floor.

Five drinks and five hours later, we are still dancing. My feet are killing me, but this is the most fun I have had in a while. James's friends are with us. They are a fun group of guys and so nice. I'm thrilled to be out and meeting new people.

Around one in the morning, we all decide to call it a night. We grab our coats that are stacked up high on a nearby chair. We head outside to catch our cabs. I'm tipsy, but James gets me a cab before getting his own. I hug everyone, wish them goodnight, and head home. I give the driver my address as I lay back against the leather seat. This has been such a great night!

Thirty minutes later I'm home, my makeup is off, and I'm in my bed. I text James and tell him how much fun I had. He responds right away saying we should all go again another Friday. I respond *"yes"* and put my phone down. I settle down into my bed, and I fall asleep right away.

I'm slightly hungover the next morning. I knew I would be, but that's okay. It's to be expected after all those cheap, sugary drinks. I crawl out of bed. The wood floor is cold beneath my feet, and I wince. My feet are still sore from all the dancing.

I walk out into the living room, and the apartment is quiet. David has left for the weekend. I don't want to sit alone in my apartment all day. I grab my phone from the bedroom that is charging by my bed. I see a text from David saying he has left and will be home tomorrow evening. I sit on my bed and text him back. I scroll through my phone to find Jillian's number that I stored a few days earlier.

I sit and think for a few minutes as to what I'm going to say. Why am I so awkward? Just send her a casual text and ask her if she wants to meet up or something.

Happy Saturday! What are you up to? If you are not busy, do you want to meet on Michigan Ave to shop for a bit?

I put the phone down and walk to the bathroom to start getting ready for the day. A few minutes later, my phone beeps. I finish brushing my teeth and walk through the kitchen and living room and into my bedroom. There's a message from Jillian.

Sure! What time?

I look at the time. It's ten-thirty.

How is around noon at Michigan and Chicago Ave?

Jillian lives in the Gold Coast, and I can get off the train at the Red Line and walk over to meet her. In the kitchen, I fill a glass with cold water, take two Advil, then take a nice hot shower. I'm happy to have some plans so I won't be sitting in the house all day. Having something to do will also help me push through my hangover. I slip on a navy-blue sweater, jeans, and head back to the bathroom to do my makeup and straighten my hair.

Forty minutes later, I'm ready to shop. I leave my apartment and start my short walk to the Brown Line. As I walk up the stairs to the platform, I remember that I can switch to the Red Line at Fullerton, which is the next stop on the Brown line. I'm starting to get this whole train thing. It feels good. I adjust my scarf and zip up my coat. Standing outside in the cold is the worst. I see down the track that the train is coming. A minute later the train arrives, and I get on and take the quick ride over to Fullerton. I get off the train just as the Red Line comes into the station. I quickly get onto the Red Line and take the ten-minute train ride downtown to the Chicago Avenue stop.

It's my first time getting off the train at Chicago Avenue, and I quickly realize that I'm in a busy part of the city. I pause to figure out where to go. People are pushing past me. There are four different exits, and I look around at each one. I have no idea which stairs to take. I pick what I think sounds right and slowly walk up the dirty train station stairs.

At the top, I see a McDonald's sign. I move to the side of the sidewalk so I can figure out which direction to go. I turn around. I don't see much west on Chicago Avenue, at least nothing that looks like the direction of Michigan Avenue. I turn back around and start walking toward what I think is the right direction. I reach the next street and see a street sign that says, Wabash. Yay! I did it! I'm so proud that I have taken the train all by myself to downtown, and I don't even feel that nervous. I find myself smiling at that accomplishment.

I reach the Park Hyatt hotel and decide that this is a good place to text Jillian. I let her know that I'm here. She responds a minute later with a *"be right there."* I stand under the heat lamp to keep warm and watch the shoppers pass by. I hear my name and realize Jillian is standing next to me. I was watching two ladies walk by. Each was wearing beige wool coats and beautiful designer bags. Where do they get clothes like that? I notice that Jillian is also wearing an over-sized leopard-print faux fur coat and tall flat black boots.

"You in dreamland or something?"

"Nope. Sorry!" I quickly snap back to reality. "You ready to go do some shopping? I really need a pair of better boots. Something that I can wear to walk around in that will also be okay for the snowy weather."

I looked down at my heeled boots. "These are just not great for walking around the city, and they'd be terrible in the snow."

"Oh, no, you can't wear those! You will literally slip and slide all over the place."

"Okay, where do you think we should go? I'll just follow you!"

"Well, since we are close, let's start at Macy's. Then we can head down Michigan Avenue."

"Okay, sounds good to me!"

I tell her about my fun night at *SoPo* with James. I suggest that we should all go sometime. "I'd love to go," she says. But I know that with or without her, I'm definitely planning on going again.

As I open the large door to Macy's, a family of four pushes through from inside. The parents look miserable, and as they drag their kids out of the store. I give Jillian a look. We step to one side and happily let them through. The store is packed with shoppers. We stroll through the first floor and head up to the shoe department. It's huge, but I don't see much that I like. It's near the end of boot season. I think it's going to be difficult to find something.

"Okay, let's go. I'm not seeing anything I like here. Let's just walk down Michigan and see what we can find."

A few minutes later we are back outside into the cold and heading down busy Michigan Avenue.

"So, last night I attended an event for *Second City Style*. One of the boutiques in the Gold Coast was having an event."

"Really? That sounds fun! Did you go with friends?"

"No, just me."

"Oh. Don't you get nervous going alone?"

"No, I'm used to it. I usually end up knowing someone anyways. It's fun of course, and I like it, but I know the routine now. You go, have some champagne, engage in some small talk, take some photos, and you leave."

"Still. Just going to an event like that sounds really fun and like something you would see in the movies."

"Well, they are not always that glamorous. Like I said the other day, I promise, you will get to go sometime."

"Well, I can't wait!"

We pass a shoe store and decide to head inside. The store is full of gorgeous leather boots. I should be looking for something practical, but I instantly set my eyes on a pair of cognac knee-high boots. The color and style are just perfect. I know if I get a pair like these,

I would have them for a long time. I pick up one boot and look at the bottom to see the price tag. They are $198, so I better really, really like them. I have never in my life thought about buying such an expensive pair of boots.

Before I can change my mind, I ask the sales associate if they have my size and, of course, they do. I turn around and look at Jillian.

"Well, let's hope they look terrible."

Jillian gives me a look. We both know that couldn't possibly be true. The sales associate brings the box over to me, and I try them on. It's just what I was afraid of. These boots are gorgeous! The leather is soft, and they fit perfectly. They have a slight wedge, which is not ideal for walking around, but they feel more comfortable than my heeled boots. I should be shopping for flat, waterproof boots that are good for walking around the city. But, I love my heels and wedges. I'm apprehensive about making such a big purchase, since these boots are also a big chunk of my paycheck, but they are real city girl chic boots! I've seen so many girls walking around wearing boots like these, and I just *have* to have them.

I take a few minutes to walk around and look at a few other pairs that are more practical. By comparison, they just seem so boring. The color and style of those other boots are so nice.

"I should just get these plain black boots."

"Yeah, you can. But you could probably order a pair like that online for way less. Those cognac boots are really in right now. I actually just wrote a piece for the blog on stylish winter-to-spring boots and those boots are totally it. Plus, the wedge is not that high. You can definitely walk in them, just not miles."

"Okay. I'm sold. Now I feel like I need some nicer clothes, shoes, and accessories. Everyone walks around with these gorgeous coats, scarves, and boots, and I feel like my style is so basic and…"

"Not a city style?"

"Yes. I know it might sound silly, but I want to look good and to fit in."

"No. I get it. Style and fashion are a big part of the city, and you will find your style. Especially after you have been here for a few seasons."

"Okay. Let me go pay."

I grab the box and head to the counter. I also purchased the leather spray so I can make them somewhat waterproof. After tax and the leather spray, I leave the store with my brand-new city boots and $227.82 on my credit card.

I promise myself that I won't charge anything else. I will pay half now and half next month. This sounds like a good plan. I feel better already. I didn't have practical boots, but I had the perfect "city girl" boots. If it snows again, I will just figure something out. I can also order a pair of black flat boots online, just as Jillian suggested and save these for when I'm going out.

I'm happy with my purchase and my plan. We're on Michigan Avenue again, and it's cold, so we decide to warm up and grab a coffee and sandwich from Starbucks. Starbucks has pretty good sandwiches, and that would mean lunch would only cost me about ten dollars. After my expensive purchase, a cheap lunch sounds good to me.

We pass the Ralph Lauren store on our way to Starbucks, and I notice the *RL Restaurant* that we passed earlier. It's so charming with its big, wooden French-style doors and blue awning. It seems the perfect cozy spot on a frigid day. It's a part of Ralph Lauren, and I figured it might be a pricey place for lunch.

"What's that *RL* place like?"

"Oh, that's a great place to go. You would really like it. Very cozy and tons of charm. They have good grilled cheese and tomato soup. Do you want to go there instead?"

I do, and it sounds amazing. But I think it's best to stick to the plan and just go to Starbucks.

"No, it's okay, we can save it for another day."

We cross Chicago Avenue, walk through the park past the historic Water Tower, then head left toward the Gold Coast. I love how quaint and beautiful this neighborhood is. We pass by Aritzia, Barneys, and Hermès. It's so much fun to window shop. As we walk by, Jillian tells me there's also a fabulous lunch spot in Barneys called

Freds. She says they have the best salads and a quaint little outdoor patio in the summer. We head inside Starbucks, and we each order a hot drink; a white mocha for me, and a chai latte for Jillian, along with two sandwiches.

We look for an open table while we wait for our drinks. This Starbucks has two levels, and it's really cozy. We are lucky enough to find a table upstairs, close to the fireplace. We enjoy our sandwiches and drinks as we chat about work. We talk about how fun the other guys are in the office and how crazy some of our clients can be.

"Speaking of crazy, what do you think about Mark? He's always just parading around the office. But he doesn't seem to do much. He definitely doesn't work as hard as the rest of us."

"I agree, he's also not around much either. It's very strange."

We switch the subject to the upcoming company outing, which we are both excited for if the team reaches our goal for February. We are ahead of schedule already, so everyone in the office is motivated to reach this month's goal.

We finish our lunch, and I look at my phone and see that it's almost four. Jillian is going out with a guy that she sees regularly, but she says it's nothing really that serious. To me, she seems a little guarded, and I wonder what her story truly is?

"Okay, well thanks for texting me, Kelly. It was fun to go shopping for shoes. I should head home to relax for a bit before I have to get ready."

"Yeah, let's go. Thanks for going with me. It was fun."

We both stand up and throw our garbage away. I make sure I have my new purchase, and we head toward the door.

"Okay, Jillian. See you on Monday! Have fun tonight."

"Thanks, see ya."

I cross the street and head toward State Street. I make a left on State to head toward the Red Line station.

It's almost dark by the time I get off the train. It's okay. There are plenty of people around heading out for Saturday night. I didn't care either that I'm going home to an empty apartment. It has been a great weekend so far, and I didn't feel as lonely as I did before. My attitude has definitely changed, and it is really paying off. I felt good about everything. I look forward to seeing how things will change even more for me over the next few months.

I really do believe that if you want to make things better, you can. Sometimes, it is just about going after what you really want to do and having a positive attitude.

I make some tea and popcorn, put on my pajamas, curl up on my couch, and turn on the TV to watch a sappy Hallmark movie. I just love these movies, they are such a good, guilty pleasure.

SIX

I wake up Sunday morning just before nine with a text from my brother saying he's heading back to the city in a few hours. His friend, Crystal, is going to drive him back, so he doesn't have to take the train. He is going to her house first because she has something to show him. I decide to clean the house a little and get my laundry done.

Around one in the afternoon, I hear two people walking up the stairs and figure it was my brother and Crystal. David bursts through the front door, his bag in tow with Crystal right behind him. I give him a big hug. I smile at Crystal and notice she is grinning and holding something tiny in her hands. It is a little black and white kitten and he or she is adorable!

"Is that your kitten? It's so cute! Why did you bring it here?"

"Well, umm, my Dad was in the yard and noticed this tiny little thing. He walked over to it thinking it was a mouse or something and realized it was this kitten. He brought it inside because it was so cold outside. We couldn't believe she had survived out there. We warmed her up and later that day, took her to the vet.

The vet said she was fine and healthy, and we wondered where she had come from? We checked with a few neighbors around us, but they said they weren't missing a kitten.

I want to keep her, but our cat is so mean to her. She's so tiny. I don't want her scared or hurt. So, I asked David if I could bring her here to see if you would take her for a bit until I find someone who wants her. She's so sweet, and David said it is up to you. So here she is."

Crystal hands me the tiny kitten, and I cradle her in my arms. She is such a sweet little thing, but I don't want the responsibility of a cat right now.

"Ugh, Crystal, I don't know. I don't want to take care of a kitten right now."

"It won't be for long. I promise! I brought you all her things. You just might need some more food, litter, and a litter box."

I sit down on the couch, and the kitten immediately curls up in a little ball in my lap.

"Okay, fine. Little kitty can stay for a few days. But, I don't want a pet right now. So, you need to find her a home."

Crystal looks over at me and smiles. "Yay! Great! Thank you so much! Okay, well I should really start heading back home. I will keep you guys posted and try to find a home for her asap. Thank you, guys, so much for taking her."

"You're welcome. It's no problem."

"Well, Okay, I'll see you guys soon."

Crystal gives us each a hug and heads out the door. I told her having the kitten is no problem, but I'm really not happy about this. I've never had a cat, and I have no idea what to do with one. David closes the door behind her and comes over to sit with me on the couch.

"Kelly, I'm so sorry about this. I didn't know what else to do. She kind of trapped me when she told me to come over this morning. She asked me if we could take her in front of her family, and I felt like I didn't have a choice."

"It's okay. We'll figure it out. I think we should go to the store soon to get kitty whatever she needs. She might have to use the bathroom or something?"

I just bought those expensive boots, so I'm already feeling guilty having to put more money on my credit card. Hopefully, the things we need to get for the kitten won't cost too much. I decide now would also be the time to have a little chat with my brother. We put the kitty in a blanket on the dining room chair. She looks so cozy.

"Well, David, she's definitely a sweet little thing."

"She is, she looks like a little cow cat."

We throw on our coats and shoes and head out the front door. We walk toward the Petco on Halsted Street. I take a deep breath and think about how to start the conversation.

"So, David, what's going on with you lately? You don't seem to like it here. You have made plans to go home every weekend."

He doesn't say anything, so I continue.

Also, what's going on with the job situation? You know you need to get one soon. I can't pay all the rent by myself. Why can't you just get a serving job in the meantime?"

"I don't want to serve. I want to get a job as a personal trainer."

"I know. But, you could make good money and still look for what you want to do."

I can tell he's starting to get annoyed. I don't want to sound like I'm nagging, and I really don't want this to turn into a fight. So, I change my tone.

"Okay, listen. I'm sure you will find something soon. I have no doubt you will get the job you want. Keep being positive and maybe just look into some other options."

I feel a little annoyed that we can't talk more about this. I am nervous that I'm going to have to pay next month's rent. Spending the whole amount will really hurt my bank account and will make things financially difficult for me.

We get what we need from Petco and walk back home. Things are quiet between us on the way back to our apartment. We head back up the stairs and walk inside only to find the little kitten still sitting in the blanket on the dining room chair.

"Awe! How cute is she! She didn't even move the whole time we were gone!"

I set up a place for her food and litter box. I pick her up and show her where her food, water, and litter are. We spend the rest of the day hanging out with our new little guest. David doesn't bring up our last conversation, and neither do I. The little kitten is a good distraction and breaks the ice after our talk. Hopefully, he will get a few interviews this week and figure it out.

Later in the evening, as we are watching more episodes of *The Office*, the tiny kitten is curled up and cozy my lap.

I look over at my brother. "So, should we call her Sophie or Gracie?"

"I like Gracie."

"Yeah, me too. Sweet little Gracie."

SEVEN

My alarm goes off. It's Monday morning again. Don't you feel like it's always Friday and then before you know it, it's Monday again? I feel that way. I didn't sleep well last night. Little Gracie was climbing around and exploring my room most of the night. She is more active during the nighttime than during the day. However, I finally got her to settle down around two in the morning. I decided to let her snuggle in bed with me. She soon fell asleep next to me, and she seemed really content after that.

Today, I'm wearing my new boots, because it's a dreary day, and I need something to get me going. I'm on the train, feeling more tired than usual. I need to get my morning coffee from Starbucks. I look around the train. I think everyone feels the way I do. Tired.

I'm downtown now, and fog is hanging low around the buildings. People are keeping their heads down as they make their way into their buildings. I guess this is what you would call the *dead of winter*.

I walk into Starbucks and get into a long line. I have about ten minutes to be at work. The line is always so much longer on Monday mornings. I should know this by now.

I give my order and try to be friendly as possible to the morning crew. I'm waiting for my coffee at the end of the bar, and I hear my name called out. The other customers in line are not very friendly this morning, and I feel like someone has to be. I tell them all to have a good day.

I push through the glass doors of the office and see that Vin is at his desk. He is early. He usually doesn't come in until around nine-thirty. He looks up and motions for me to come back. Ugh! Not today. I want to get settled and drink some coffee. I put my stuff down and slowly walk toward his office.

"Hi, Kelly. How was your weekend?"

I have been in such a funk this morning that I forgot that I did have a great weekend.

"Oh, we had a fun time at *SoPo*. We should all go sometime."

"Yeah. Maybe."

"How was yours?"

"It was fine. So anyway. I got here early this morning to go over all our projects for this month. We are way ahead of schedule, and I think we will meet our goal."

"That is great."

"So, with that said, as one of your responsibilities, I would like you to come up with some ideas for the company outing."

"Okay. I can do that."

"Great. I will speak to James, so he can get things organized on his side. I will give you a budget, and you can start planning something for all of us. It can be during work hours as well. We can all take a half day, maybe on the last day of the month, which I think is a Friday."

"Perfect! I will start looking at some ideas."

I walk out of his office and annoy the guys by saying my morning hellos to everyone. No one seems to be in a good mood today, so I walk back to my desk.

I spend the morning working on the new project that James has given me. I take a short break to instant message James and Jillian, so I can tell them about my brother bringing the cat home. They both think it's crazy that Crystal would bring a cat over and ask me to take it. They ask if I'm going to keep her? I tell them I that I didn't want a cat at all, but she is so sweet. I don't think I could give her up now. I have instantly grown attached to her. I have been wondering most of the day how she is doing.

I'm excited to rush home to make sure Gracie is okay. I get off the train. I walk as fast as I can toward my apartment. With my keys ready, I rush up the stairs and fumble as I try to unlock the door. I swing the door open and hear a little meow. Gracie is walking over to me from the couch. I pick her up and do a quick look around the apartment to make sure she hasn't had any accidents. I can't see anything. I cuddle her and tell her she is such a good little girl. Maybe having a cat will be super easy after all. It seems you don't have to train them like a dog.

The apartment is quiet, so my brother must be out. I send him a quick text asking him where he is and what he wants to do for dinner. While waiting for his response, I walk into the kitchen to see what I can make. We don't have much left in the way of groceries. We must make a trip to the store soon. It would be so much easier to have a car. I missed my car. I had to sell it because I couldn't afford to also have a car payment right now. I do miss being able to run to the store for anything, whenever you need something. I should ask the girls at work what they do when they need groceries.

My brother walks in about a half hour later. He looks a lot happier than he has in the last few weeks.

"What have you been up to today?"

"Well, I was downtown applying for a position at the Starbucks at the Palmer House Hilton."

"Oh really? Why Starbucks?"

There was nothing wrong with working at Starbucks. But I just figured he would make more money serving.

"Well, Starbucks is franchised by the hotel. So, if you work at the hotel's Starbucks, you have a better chance at other opportunities to work in different departments within the hotel."

"What do you want to do at the hotel?"

"Well, I went to the hotel because I'm interested in their private health club. It looks amazing, and it's open to both hotel guests and locals. However, the club is not hiring now, but the manager said Starbucks is. If I get a job there, I have a better chance at getting into the health club."

I'm thrilled that he has spent the day doing something productive. I guess my little chat helped to motivate him to go and do something.

"That's so great! I'm sure you will get it."

"Yeah, I hope so. It's something, and Starbucks pays okay, and it gets me in the door of what I want to do."

I feel so much better about our situation. If David gets this job soon, he will be able to pay his half of the rent. I'm keeping my fingers crossed!

It's late on Wednesday afternoon, and an instant message pops up. *Hey, Kelly, come over here.* It's from Amy. *Okay, be right there.* I walk over to the three girls.

"Hey girls. What's up?"

"Hey! We have been chatting, and we are all free tomorrow night if you want to go out for drinks after work? We keep meaning to make plans but then the weeks fly by."

"Yeah, that sounds good to me, I'm free."

I must admit I'm excited to go out with these girls. They seem nice, and they're a lot like me. I think we all have a lot in common.

"Okay, great." chimes in Kourtney. How about we go to *Pops for Champagne* for drinks? We can walk there. It's only about a fifteen-minute walk from here."

"I haven't been there yet, but it sounds like a fun place." As I finish my sentence, I feel someone is behind me.

"What's going on girls?"

It's Mark. He's making his afternoon rounds, trying to seem super important.

"Oh, nothing much," I say. "Okay, I'll talk to you girls later." I walk away and head back to my desk.

On Thursday morning, I rush around like a lunatic trying to figure out what to wear. I have to dress for the work day, but I want to make sure I still look cute for drinks this evening. Kourtney always has the best clothes. She always looks so sophisticated, and everything she wears seems to fit her so well. She told me she gets most of her clothes from Nordstrom and at a few of her favorite boutiques in the city. I haven't shopped at Nordstrom, but I should go soon because I would love to have a few new staples to update my closet.

I finally decide on a blue-ish purple long tunic sweater, black leggings, and an old pair black boots. I would wear my new cognac boots, but they don't quite go with my sweater, and I don't have time to change. I look in the mirror at my outfit. It's somewhat cute. My sweater is newer than some of my others. It's okay for work and good enough for getting drinks after work. I hope work goes by quickly because I'm looking forward to this evening. I did a Google search for *Pops for Champagne* last night. It looks like a chic cocktail and champagne bar.

Through the glass doors, I see Amy is already at her desk. I walk over to say good morning.

"Hey. You are here early, how is everything going?"

"Fine. Just trying to hire a few more models for our big event coming up. Mark is starting to put the pressure on me to have all the models booked and placed. It's our biggest event yet, and I want everything to go well. We have all been working so hard on this."

"Yeah, I see that."

"So, Kelly, do you want to be a model for the night?" Amy looks up me and smiles as she plays with her long hair.

"Umm, thanks, but no thanks. No offense to the models but I'm not passing out shots and wearing tiny shorts. It's not my thing."

It's early afternoon. I'm at my desk when out of the corner of my eye I see a short girl with short dark hair storming through the glass doors with a bunch of flowers in her hands.

"Is Vin here?" Her eyes are darting around as she is looking to see if she can spot him first.

I know exactly who this is. It's Vin's current girlfriend, and she looks just like he described her. I'm usually not one to not like some-one, but this girl seems terrible. Vin must have seen her come in because he's quickly at my desk. He whisks her back down to his office, and I hear the door close shut.

I quickly get up from my desk and walk over to the girls.

"Is that who I think it is? The three girls nod their heads at me.

"Geez! She seems super friendly! There's something about her that doesn't seem right. She seems so angry, and Vin is so not like that."

Natalie looks up from her computer. "I completely agree with you. She has come in here a few times over the past few months, and she is unfriendly like that every time."

"Well, she sure did startle me when she barged in like that. She seems like an angry person."

I head back to my desk. A few minutes later, I hear Vin's office door open. His girlfriend storms right past my desk. I glance at her, and she shoots me a dirty look. She grabs the handles on the glass doors, looks to her left, and gives the girls the same look. She walks out, lets the glass door slam behind her, and just like that, she's gone. I type in my instant messenger to all three girls.

Thank goodness!

I feel someone coming up behind me, and I quickly close my instant messenger. I spin around, and it's Vin with the flowers.

"Can you find vases for these in the kitchen?"

"Sure!" He doesn't look happy. "So, why the flowers?"

"Oh, she thought they would be nice to brighten up the office. She just wanted to stop by for a second to see me."

"Oh, that's so nice."

"Yeah, I guess so."

Vin hands me the flowers and walks off. I get up from my desk and walk past the girls toward the kitchen.

"He doesn't look happy," I mumble to them.

I find two vases and fill both with water. I unwrap the flowers and lay them all out on the counter. As I cut the flowers, I think about Vin and can't help but feel bad for him. He's such a nice guy, but his mood instantly changed when she came in. He is not happy with her. However, this is not any of my business. I finish cutting the flowers and arrange them in the vases. I walk around the office trying to figure out where the flowers should go. I decide to put one vase in the conference room and the other one on the front edge of my desk.

At five o'clock the girls yell over that they will be ready in a few minutes, so I wrap up my work. I check my hair and touch up my makeup at my desk. Fifteen minutes later all four of us are walking out onto Michigan Avenue.

The street is overflowing with business people who are heading home for the day. There is also the usual tourist traffic, and there is always someone who is trying to figure out where they are going to next. I follow the girls as we weave in and out of the crowd. I'm learning that in the city, you have to keep moving and try not get in anyone's way. We pass the Wrigley Building, The Shops at North-bridge, and once we get to Ohio Street, we all turn left and walked a few short blocks to *Pops for Champagne*.

The inside of *Pops* looks just like the online photos I saw last night. Tables line the perimeter of the restaurant next to the windows, and a large bar is in the middle. There's plenty of seating around the bar. At some of the tables, there's a few girls chatting and sipping their drinks. They obviously came here straight from work. We are seated at a table right by the window overlooking State Street.

As we take off our coats and sit down, a busboy is at our table filling our water glasses. I open the drink menu and see about a hundred different types of champagne ranging from roughly one hundred dollars a bottle to seven hundred dollars a bottle. Whoa! Hopefully, the girls don't want to split one of those. I had no idea this place is so expensive. I turn to the cocktail and wine list page and see that they have some wines and champagnes by the glass as well as some signature cocktails. Okay, this sounds more like it. I spot a Bellini that sounds delicious, and I close the menu.

A waiter comes over to introduce himself and asks to take our order. The girls choose a glass of wine, and I order my fancy little Bellini cocktail. He takes the menus and walks off.

"So, you guys." Natalie flips hair her back and leans into the table. "Wasn't that so crazy in the office today. I can't believe Vin's girlfriend comes in and acts like that to all of us. Doesn't she know how rude she is? Do you think Vin knows how rude she is?"

"Probably. When he came to my desk with the flowers, he seemed pretty annoyed."

Natalie looks directly at me. "Do you think? He never says anything about her to me. I also don't ask him either. I wonder what she said to him in the office? She sure stormed out looking mad today."

"I have no idea. It's really not our business, right?"

"No. But it's a little uncomfortable for everyone when she comes in."

"Yep. It is, and probably for Vin as well."

A few minutes later we get our drinks, and I have to say my Bellini looks delicious!

"Kelly, ugh, I should have gotten your drink. It looks so good." Amy looks down at her wine glass. "I always order white wine because it's easy."

"Well, just order a Bellini next." Amy picks up her wine to take a sip, and I quickly put out my hand to stop her. "Wait! Should we all say 'cheers'? Thanks for arranging this, guys."

We all lift our glasses for cheers and take a sip of our drinks. I'm curious to get to know these girls other than our small talk in the office, so I start asking questions.

"So, Kourtney, where are you from? Have you been in Chicago for long?"

"Well, I'm from New York City. I just moved here in October to be with my fiancé. He has a great job in finance. I actually got lucky and found my job with the agency working on the model side a few weeks after we moved here."

"Oh, really. That is lucky. So where do you guys live?"

"We live in River North at Kingsbury Plaza. It's a high-rise, and it's a really nice building."

"Oh really?"

"Yep. I love the building. It has a ton of great amenities too. Our rent is kind of high, but it doesn't even compare to what we paid in New York."

"So, you like Chicago then?"

"I like Chicago, it's way cheaper. We would never live in a luxury building in New York. But I love New York."

"So, do you think you will go back to New York."

"Maybe, someday. It all depends on my fiancé's job."

"Gotcha. Okay, so Amy what about you? I'm just curious about you guys. So sorry about all the questions."

"No, it's okay. I want to hear about you too Kelly. I'm originally from Michigan. I've been in Chicago for just over a year. I only live a few blocks over from here, on the other side of Michigan Avenue, explains Amy. "Have you heard of the Streeterville neighborhood?"

"No, I haven't."

"Well, it's the neighborhood just east of Michigan Avenue. I live over on McClurg and Ohio Street. I love the neighborhood because it's so close to everything. Especially all the shopping on Michigan Avenue. I can also take the train or the bus and get anywhere I want in the city."

"Yeah, that is so nice! I know the area. I just never knew what it was called. It's my dream to live over there. Do you live alone?"

"No, I live with my boyfriend who is also from Michigan."

"Do you think you guys will stay in Chicago?"

"I'm not sure. I love Chicago, but I miss my family in Michigan."

"Yeah, being away from family is really hard. Natalie, do you live around here too?"

"No, I live in Lincoln Park."

"Oh cool. I live in Lakeview. Do you have a boyfriend too?"

"Yeah, I moved here after college with him. We don't get along that well anymore. He's boring. He never wants to go out or do anything with me. He just hangs out at home."

"Oh, that's too bad. I'm so sorry."

"Yeah, it sucks. I'm going to move out, I think, when our lease is up. I love Chicago, and I just wish I had someone who wanted to go out and do more."

"I'm really sorry to hear that. I hope things do get better for you."

I give Natalie a smile. I totally understand now why she wants to hang out with Vin. He's a nice guy and seems to be a lot of fun. I don't bring up the topic of Vin, and I switch the conversation over to fashion. I need some advice from the girls on how to dress for the city.

First things first, what shoes should I be wearing? I am starting to get a little insecure about the silliest things, and I have no idea why the shoe thing is such a big deal to me. However, if anyone can help me feel better, it will be Kourtney. She has the best style and seems to know these things. Surely, she would know what I should shop for each season. Plus, she's from New York City. You have to walk around everywhere in New York.

"So, guys. You might think this is strange, but I need your help with some fashion advice. I love wearing my heels to work, but I can't walk around in them all day. When I lived in the suburbs, I would wear cute shoes all the time, and it was never an issue. Since I've moved here, my feet are killing me, and I'm ruining all my shoes. I don't know what shoes to buy that won't hurt my feet while I'm out and about. I'm doing much more walking now."

I stop and look at them. The girls are staring right at me as though I said something weird. Okay, maybe it did sound weird.

"I know. You all think I'm strange."

Kourtney smiles at me. "That's so funny. You're not strange. It's just funny to hear you seem so upset about shoes. I think we've all been there. You don't get to hear all our random conversations in the office. I feel like there needs to be a city manual."

She stops and looks around as though she is about to tell me something top secret. She puts her long hair behind her ears and then she continues.

"Okay, first, get some cute flats or tennis shoes. They are popular now and everyone is wearing them. They look good with pretty much anything. I think flats are more in style than heels if you ask me. If you want to wear heels, just bring a pair or leave a pair at work to change into."

"Really. Hmm, I can't believe I don't own a pair of flats. I've seen women wear them, and I can't believe I've never thought to wear them myself. That seems like such a simple solution."

"Well, in the summer it's what everyone wears. I promise. People will actually look at you weird if you are walking around in heels."

I blush a little thinking about all the times I've struggled in my heels.

"Also, you must invest in a pair of really nice flat leather boots for the fall and winter. You can get them fixed every year at a shoe repair if they are good quality. For snowy weather, get a pair of snow boots. There is no way around it. It's a must in the city. I like Sorel. They last forever, and they are super stylish. You must invest in a few nice pairs of shoes that you can wear over and over each season. Remember when shopping for anything, classic pieces never go out of style."

I look at the girls, and they're nodding their heads in agreement. How did I not know all of this! I feel so dumb!

"Wow, thank you. You guys are the best. I guess it's time to invest in some good pieces to help me survive the city." I cringe when I think about my credit card and adding more money to my growing balance.

It might sound silly, but I think advice like this would be helpful to other girls who are new to Chicago. I hope to help others one day because the city is overwhelming. It is like starting over. You not only need to learn how to navigate the city, but you also need to learn how to adjust to city life. It's hard to meet new people, and let's be honest, everyone wants to fit in. I can't believe I didn't know any of this. I love fashion and styling outfits. Her advice seems so simple. I knew I had so much to learn and not just about what to wear.

I look at my phone, and it's just after eight. We finish up our second drink and the small bites we've shared. We split the bill, and after tip, it was just over $60 each. Yikes! I put down my credit card again. I'm starting to feel as though I can barely survive on my salary. I can't afford to go out like this all the time. It sure is expensive to have fun in Chicago. I need to figure out a better way to budget my life. This evening, however, was fun with the girls. I'm glad I got to know them all a little better, and I'm kind of bummed the evening is already over.

From the backseat of my cab, I look out the window as we drive down Michigan Avenue and onto Lake Shore Drive. The streets are not as crowded as earlier, and the buildings' lights are beautiful. I must admit that with each passing day, I'm beginning to feel more and more like I belong in this city.

EIGHT

It's the last week of the month and guess what! We are about to meet our team goal! Everyone is so excited. Vin told me I can go ahead and get tickets for a Bulls game. I offered everyone a few suggestions, and this is what the majority of the office wants to do. I'm okay with this idea. I have never been to a Bulls game, and it sounds like a lot of fun. We are planning to leave the office early on Friday, so we can have a few drinks and get something to eat somewhere in the West Loop before the game starts at seven.

I'm busy working on a new project when I hear my phone beep and see that I have a text from my brother.

Hey! I got the job at Starbucks at the hotel! I start training on Friday.

OMG! Yay! Congrats! I'm so proud of you! I know this is not actually what you want, but it's definitely a step toward what you want to do! Should we go somewhere fun to celebrate tonight?

Thank you! Okay. Should we meet at Lao Sze Chuan? I'm craving the Tony's Chicken and the Crispy Shrimp.

Yes! Yum! That sounds perfect! We might have to get the crab rangoons too! I'll see you later then!

I wake up on Friday excited not only about the upcoming weekend but also about leaving work early to go a Bulls game. It has been a long week. I have been working hard to gain more responsibilities other than just being the receptionist. My days are hectic now which I enjoy. I want to prove to myself that I can learn as much as I can about digital marketing, web development, and SEO. I find it all very interesting and every day I'm learning something new. However, having a shorter day today will be a nice break and fun way to start the weekend.

I peek through the window and see it's snowing like crazy. Oh no! What am I going to do? I don't have snow boots. Kourtney was so right. I need to and should have invested in a good pair of snow boots. It's a total mess outside. I glance at my choices of shoes in my tiny bedroom. They're all under my rolling rack, which is now actually taped to my wall because it's so heavy with all my clothes. I see my shiny, new cognac boots. I have been lucky throughout January and most of February that there hasn't been much snow. There is no way I can wear those boots today. They will get destroyed. Sigh. I walk out and head to the bathroom.

The bathroom door is shut, and the light is on. I call out to my brother.

"David?"

"Almost done."

I forgot he is starting his new job today. I'm not going to ask him how much longer since it's his first day but for me, every minute counts. I'm so slow in the morning and getting to work today isn't going to be easy. I wander back to my room and decide what I'm going to wear while I'm waiting. I don't think I have to get dressed up today, so I decide on a cozy gray sweater and dark denim jeans. I walk back to the bathroom and knock gently.

"Hey. How are you feeling?"

"Okay."

"Are you nervous?"

"A little. But the manager that I'm training with seems really cool."

"That's good." I give him the same pep talk he gave to me on my first day of work.

"You know, in a few days, you won't feel as nervous. Everyone feels the same way on the first day."

"Yep. I know. I told you that."

I don't ask any more questions because he obviously doesn't want to make small talk. Two minutes later he is out of the bathroom. He gives me a quick hug and walks into his room.

"Good Luck!" I call out to him.

"Thanks!"

I choose an old pair of boots I bought from Target that I forgot about. They're pretty worn and old. They are not snow boots, but if they get ruined, it will be okay. I'm out the door and into the snow.

It's a terrible commute to downtown. The trains are late and slow, and everyone looks so miserable standing out in the snow. I'm trying to cover my face on the train platform, so I don't get raccoon eyes from the snow blowing into my face.

Once off the train, I stop by Starbucks to get coffee to warm up. I will officially be late for work. I have never been late, but I think today it will be okay. I walk into the office at 9:07 and I see that half the office is not even here yet. I guess that's to be expected when the weather is so terrible outside. However, by around nine thirty everyone is at their desks. The atmosphere is quiet, so I assume everyone is grumpy because of the weather. I am not really in the mood to get everyone's spirits up today either. Listening to music always puts me in a better frame of mind, so I put my headphones in, open my Spotify, and start my day.

Around three in the afternoon, I walk over to the team and remind them about the plans for the afternoon.

"Hey, guys! Let's start wrapping up around three-thirty so we can get over to *Green Street Meats* to have a few drinks and food before the game."

"Sounds good, thanks, Kelly. You guys hear her? Let's wrap up for the day in the next thirty minutes."

The guys mumble back an okay.

"Alright James. Make sure they are ready."

Vin is finishing up a call with a client and tells me he'll get a cab and meet us in a little bit. The rest of us walk out onto Michigan

Avenue and sidewalk is covered in salt, snow, and slush. We tromp through all the wet mess over to Lake Street and get into our cabs. I realize now why snow boats are so important, this is just so horrible to walk through, even for a few minutes.

There's already traffic in this late afternoon. The one thing I've heard about living in the city is that the weather doesn't stop people from doing what they want to do.

Green Street Meats has a massive bar in the middle with picnic style tables all around the restaurant. You wait in line to order your food, pick it up, and find an area to sit. Easy enough. It's your typical BBQ restaurant, wood-paneled walls, low-hanging lights, and kitschy decorations.

We order our drinks first before ordering our food. Most of the team orders beers but I order a margarita and sit down next to James and Jillian. I send my brother a quick text to remind him of my plans for this evening.

Hey! How was your first day? I can't wait to hear about it! I just wanted to let you know I will be out all evening. We have our company outing. Going to the Bulls game tonight!

It was good! Okay. Be safe.

I put my phone away and take a sip of my margarita. It's perfect. James and Jillian talk about something annoying that a client did today. I don't want to engage in or talk about work, so I listen and enjoy their conversation and sip on my drink.

I look up and see Vin walking through the door. His black wool coat is unbuttoned. He's dressed as though there's no blizzard outside. He is also wearing his good shoes. He mustn't have snow boots either. He is always dressed to the nines and looks cool but, geez, doesn't he get cold? He sees me and walks right over.

"Hey Kelly, what are you drinking?"

"Oh. Just a margarita."

"Looks good."

"You should get one."

"Nah. I'm going to get a beer or whiskey."

Vin heads over to the bar, and James gets up and follows him. I look around for Jillian. She's having a shot with two of the guys from the office. I look around for our team. Everyone is hanging out in groups, so I get up and join James and Vin at the bar.

I take a seat next to James. They're cracking up with laughter about something funny that happened with one of the clients. It's nice to see them having fun together outside the office.

"Okay. I think we're boring Kelly a little with all this."

"No, it's okay. I'm just sitting here listening."

"Well. Since we are all just hanging out and no one else is around, I want to tell you guys that I really enjoy and appreciate the two of you. I think, Kelly, you have done an excellent job the last few months. James, you are always good at everything you do."

"Awe. Thank you."

"Yeah, thanks, Vin. Appreciate it."

"I think we really work well together as a team, and I don't want to intrude on whatever you guys have going on, but it would be fun to all hang out together sometime."

James and I look at each other and start laughing.

"Vin! What are you talking about? We are not dating!"

"Oh! Okay. That's cool. I just thought . . ."

"Why would you think that?" James cuts in as he moves in to face him more closely.

"Umm, because you guys went out dancing and you guys talk and hang out all day at the office."

"Didn't you know I'm gay! I like Kelly, but I don't like her like that. However, she is all yours if you want!" He reaches over to pretend to move Vin and me closer together.

"Umm . . . that's not what I was trying to say either . . . "

James and I start cracking up. Vin is looking uncomfortable, embarrassed.

"We're just messing with you man. Of course, we can all hang out."

Once we convince Vin that we are just joking, he loosens up again. I notice some of the team is in line to order food and the line is also getting longer. I look at my phone. It's almost five-thirty. We have about an hour until we leave for the game.

"Hey, guys. Let's get some food. The line is getting longer, and I'm getting hungry."

"Okay. Let's do it."

The guys finish their drinks, and the three of us get in line for food. I order a pulled pork sandwich and coleslaw, and the guys each order ribs and few sides to share. We get our food and join the rest of the team at one of the picnic tables.

The food is delicious. I love a good pulled pork sandwich. One of the guys has ordered a round of shots for the table. Most of the guys and Jillian have already had quite a few drinks. He passes them around to us, and we make a quick toast to Vin for being such an awesome boss. In unison, we cheer to Vin and take the shot of whiskey. I try to get Jillian's attention, but she's is still hanging out with one of the guys. The more drinks they have, the closer they get. Good for her though, at least she is having fun.

I stick with James and Vin and head back to the bar after we're done eating. I order another margarita, and the guys order whiskeys.

"You know, Vin, I've never been to a Bulls game. I'm pretty excited to go."

"You haven't?"

"No. I haven't"

"The Bulls have been my favorite team since I was a kid. I love going to games, and I've always been a huge Michael Jordan fan."

"Have you been to a game, James?"

"Yeah, but only a few."

"Well, I can't wait to see what it's all about."

Just before six-thirty, Vin, James, and I round up our group, so we can get cabs and make it to the game on time. Vin told me the intro is the best. I don't want to miss this! Everyone is eager for the game. We head out around the same time and split up into cabs.

There is a sea of people at *United Center* all waiting outside to get into the stadium. I can feel the excitement as we walk up to get in line. I'm standing next to James and Vin, and I'm holding my ticket tightly in my hands. We have our tickets scanned through security and enter the stadium. I can feel the energy.

I wait with James and Vin at the concession. They each grab a beer and a glass of wine for me. I'm already feeling a little buzzed from the margaritas, but I'll sip on my wine throughout the game.

It's five minutes before seven. The crowd begins to boo the opposing team as they walk onto the court. At seven, the lights suddenly dim, and the intro music blasts through the speakers. The court spotlights turn on.

"Kelly. Watch all of this. You are going to love it." I look over at Vin, and he is grinning like a little kid.

I can feel chill bumps rush up my arms. Music blares throughout the stadium, and the crowd is deafening. I look up at the jumbotron. Animated bulls are charging down the streets of Chicago. Vin is right. This is so cool! The bulls bust through the opposing team's bus and reach the stadium. The announcer's voice booms through the speakers. "And now, here are your Chicago Bulls!" The Luvab-ulls are cheering on the team at the sidelines, and the enthusiasm of the Chicago crowd roars louder. I can feel its vibration throughout my body. The crowd grows wilder. The team players are announced one-by-one and rush onto the court and greet each other with a high-five.

"So, what did you think? Pretty cool right?"

"Vin. You were absolutely right. The intro is amazing!"

"Yeah. I've seen a lot of openings and Chicago has the best."

I have to say, I'm not a huge sports person. I don't watch a lot of sports, but I'm really enjoying this. It's fun to watch because it's a fast-paced game, and there is always something going on. Benny is Bull is a crowd favorite, and now I'm a fan as well, but the intro is my favorite part.

After the game, I decide to just head home. I'm really worn out from the week, and I don't want to drink anymore. James and Vin and some of the guys are going out, and they wait for me to get a cab.

"Thanks so much, Vin, for getting us these tickets. It was a lot of fun. A really good first game."

"Good. We will have to go again."

"For sure. Thanks, guys! Have a good rest of your night."

NINE

I'm back at work. However, I'm already looking forward to the weekend. I cannot wait to celebrate my birthday on Saturday with my friends and family in the 'burbs. I asked James and Jillian if they wanted to do a small dinner with me the following Friday. I found an Italian restaurant that isn't too far from where I live. I love Italian food, and I'm eager to try a cozy little traditional neighborhood restaurant.

By late Thursday afternoon, I'm burnt out from work. I walk over to the girls to chat with them for a few minutes, and I notice that all three of them seem stressed out. They were busily typing away on their computers.

"Hey, guys, what's wrong?"

Amy looks up at me. "Ugh! We are short a few models for tomorrow night's event at *Underground*. A few girls had to cancel, and it's too late to get models to cover them and get their paperwork in."

"Oh no, that's terrible. I'm so sorry."

"Yeah, Natalie thinks the three of us should just go and cover. We were going to be there anyway, but we didn't plan on actually working the event. We need four more girls, but three would be okay."

"Well. Can't Kelly can join us too?"

I give Natalie a look that says geez, thanks. "Umm, I'm not sure I can. I wish I could help. I have plans to go home this weekend to celebrate my birthday."

"Well, if you decide you can help us, we'll make it a fun night, we promise. We can have a few drinks to celebrate your birthday. I really don't want to tell Mark that we don't have enough girls. This is our first really big event, and I don't want him to think we can't handle it."

I let out a sigh and look at Amy. "Okay. I'll help you guys. I don't want Mark to be upset with you all. I guess I can go home Saturday morning instead."

Amy gets up from her desk and runs over to give me a huge hug. "Thank you! Thank you! This will be great! I promise you! It's only for a few hours. Just make sure to bring shorts. We just have to wear shorts and a promotional t-shirt. We will also hang out together the whole time."

"Okay. I can bring shorts. This will be an experience. That's for sure."

Friday evening, we head over from the office to the club *Underground*. We all squeeze into the back of a cab and head into the evening traffic. The event starts at seven, which is early for a club, but this is a promotional event before *Underground* opens to the general public for the night.

We have a lot to do before the event starts. The four of us quickly change into our shorts and tees and freshen up makeup and hair. We spend the next hour running around making sure everything is just right. We set up a few areas with gold balloons and gold beads as a giveaway along with some promotional swag the client provided. The waitstaff is setting up the bars and preparing the appetizer tables and trays. We check in each of the promotional models who are working the event as they arrive. They are given directions as to what they need to do throughout the evening. Amy is super organized and has a list of the model's names and what each of their jobs should be and where they should be stationed throughout the evening.

I'm trying to keep up with the three of them and to be as helpful as I can. I'm impressed. These girls are pros at this. I know they are a little stressed out, but you can't tell, and everything in the club looks great. Before the doors open, they take a few photos to add to the website and to show Mark. I think he will love how it turned out, however, you never know with him, he could be expecting celebrities to show up.

It's just after seven, and the club is filling up fast. Free drinks, free food, and free swag really draw a crowd. The four of us are hanging out in a corner making small talk as we hand out beads to the event guests. We dance a little and enjoy people-watching. The music is fantastic, and I hate to admit it, but I'm having a good time. Who knew I could have so much fun working an event.

Natalie gets a text from Vin saying that after the event, we should stop by Leg Room to meet him for a drink.

"He says he's with a couple of his friends, so it should be fun. I guess they have a table and so we can easily join them."

Amy, Kourtney, and I all give each other a look. We can see that Natalie wants to go.

"I'm not sure we should go."

Natalie gives Kourtney a look.

"Natalie, he's our boss, and I don't know if that's a good idea."

"I think it might be okay. I hung out with him last Friday." The three of them look at me, and Natalie's mouth drops wide open.

"Wait, you did?"

Now Natalie gives me a look.

"Yes, but it was our team's company party. Remember, we all left early last Friday?"

"Oh yeah, duh. He already told me about that."

I roll my eyes but don't give her any more information, and I change the subject.

"I wish you guys could go to our company events, as well. It stinks that you guys are in your own department."

"Okay. Well, if we are going to meet Vin, let's leave here around nine. I don't even think the other models will notice. They're all scheduled to work the event 'til ten, but we weren't planning to stay that long anyway. The club will take down all the balloons and clean up after they close."

Natalie gives Amy a big smile. She pulls out her phone and sends out a text to Vin that we are coming by.

Just after nine, we make a final check around the club to ensure everything is okay so we can leave. The event is already winding down. The girls and I change back into our regular clothes. We exit the club, jump into a cab, and I tell the driver "The Leg Room on Division," and we head off to toward the Gold Coast. We arrive at the Leg Room, and see a few people are standing in line outside. Natalie tells the bouncer our names, and he motions us to come in.

This club is much smaller and intimate than *Underground*. Red velvet chairs and couches with touches of animal print décor make the club feel trendy. We head toward the back, and we see Vin and his friends sitting in a roped-off area with his friends. One of his friends stands up to let us in.

"Hello, ladies. How was *Underground*? You guys were there early. I didn't think that place opened 'til later."

"It doesn't. We were doing a promotional event for work. I'm Amy." She holds out her arm to shake hands.

"Vince. Nice to meet you, Amy."

We introduce ourselves to Vince. On the couch is Vin still sitting with a drink in his hand. He seems so different in this environment. He's way more cool and relaxed, and there isn't that feel like we are hanging out with our boss. Natalie, of course, immediately sits next to him. I sit on the other side of Vin, and Amy and Kourtney sit next to me.

"So, Vin, how did you get this area? It's so nice."

"Oh, I come here all the time, so they all know me."

I give Vin a grin. "Oh, that's nice. Very VIP of you."

We give our drink orders to the waitress. Vin turns to face Kourtney, Amy, and me.

"So, how did the event go tonight?"

The three of us look over to Amy to let her take the lead.

"Oh. It went really well. It was fun. We got there with plenty of time to set up and check in all the girls. Everything looked great, and we took lots of photos."

"Good. You will have to show me the photos on Monday, and we can put them on the website."

Not one of us told him that we worked the event. Since everything turned out well, that part didn't seem necessary.

"So, what are you doing for your birthday tomorrow? These drinks are on me by the way so we can celebrate our first big event *and* your birthday."

He lifts his drink to cheers with the girls and me.

"Oh. Cheers, and thank you. I didn't even know you knew it was my birthday. I'm going home tomorrow to celebrate with my family and friends. Having a pretty chill day."

"Cool. Well, I heard you talking to James, something about your birthday."

"Oh. Yep. I invited James and Jillian to a birthday dinner next Friday. We are going to a little neighborhood Italian place called *Angelina's.*"

"I've never heard of it."

"Well, you should come with us."

"Okay. I'm free next Friday. I'll be there."

"Okay. Good."

I smile at Vin then look over at Natalie. She looks a little annoyed that he's paying attention to the three of us and not her. One of Vin's friends is talking to her, but she is trying hard to hear our conversation.

Then I realize that I have just invited my boss to my birthday dinner. I now feel a little weird about that. The three of us had fun at the bar last Friday so it will be pretty much the same group that night too. Actually, thinking about it, I really do want him to be there. It will be a lot of fun.

The rest of the night I try to focus on hanging out and dancing with Kourtney and Amy. Natalie seems annoyed. She's been trying so hard to get Vin's attention. I'm pretty sure she didn't overhear my earlier conversation with him. I don't want Natalie to think I'm trying to get in with Vin or make her jealous. If she likes him, that's okay. Vin and I can still be friends. I can honestly say I have no interest in dating or even thinking about dating my boss.

TEN

I made sure not to drink too much last night and to mainly stick with water at The Leg Room. I'm tired from getting home so late, so I'm moving slowly this morning.

My brother and I are taking the 10:40 train home this morning. We need to leave around nine, so we have enough time to catch the Brown Line to downtown, and then walk over to Union Station. We still have to get our tickets. It ended up being okay going home on Saturday instead of Friday. David is coming with me, and I don't want to leave little Gracie by herself for more than one night.

Before we leave, I pick her up and give her a big cuddle and lay her down on the couch. I double-check her food, water, and litter to make sure she will be okay.

"Be a good girl Gracie. See you tomorrow."

We both grab our bags and head out the door. It's a rush to get to the train, but we make it.

Dad picks us up from the station as usual. I see him pull over his car and get out to wait for us. We drag our bags over to him. He puts his arms out to give me a big hug.

"Happy Birthday, Boots."

"Thanks, Dad."

It feels good to see my Dad, and I'm really excited to see my Mum as well. I have so much to catch them up on. We pull up to the house and lug our bags into the kitchen. There is a pile of presents waiting for me on the table and a small birthday cake. I walk over to give Mum a big hug.

"It's so good to see you, sweetie. Happy Birthday!" I hold on to her for a few seconds.

"It's nice to be home, Mum."

"Have a seat, and I'll make you some coffee."

I sit down at the table. Dad and David join me. We chat about David's new job, what I have been up to at work, and my new work friends. I love spending this quality time with my family. We enjoy our coffee and a bit of birthday cake. I open my presents and thank them for the gifts.

"So, what do you want to do for the day?"

"Maybe we could just go shopping for a bit. Dad, you can come with us if you want? I'm not hungry after having cake for a late breakfast, but maybe we can bring home lunch from somewhere."

"Yeah. We can do that with you. Let me just clean this up."

"Okay. I'll help you. David, what are you going to do?"

"I think I will go see what Crystal is up to." He gets up from the table and walks up the stairs with his phone.

As I'm getting ready for the evening dinner with my friends, I realize that I haven't seen them for a while, which is so strange, because I used to see them most weekends. I'm looking forward to catching up with them. We used to work together at Chili's during college, so we thought that Chili's would be an easy place for us to meet up for my birthday. Margaritas and chips and salsa sounded good to me!

I walk into Chili's and feel at ease with the familiar environment. I see my group already at one of the larger tables.

"Hey, guys! So good to see you!"

"Kelly! Happy Birthday!"

"Thank you! I'm so glad we could do this, it's been awhile since we have all been together."

I slide into the table. My friend Heather gives me a hug as I sit next to her.

"Hi love, we want to hear everything you have been up to. How's the city and your new job?"

"It's been good, really good. Much better than last time I saw you guys. I changed my attitude and was determined to give the city a real try. I am enjoying work, and I have made a few new friends. We actually just did an event for work last night."

"That's so great. I'm glad you are enjoying yourself now. Last time we saw you, you did seem a little unhappy."

Louis gives me a grin. "And, I'm sure you will meet someone soon. I'm still bummed things didn't work out with you and Dylan."

"Ugh! Don't remind me about him! He was the absolute worst!"

"Well, I thought you two would be good together. Have you seen him anymore?"

"No. I haven't. Thank goodness."

"Well, he's back with his old girlfriend. I guess she recently got a job in the city."

"Oh, well that totally makes more sense why he just dropped me. Anyway, he's still a jerk, but at least I now know why he just stopped talking to me."

David takes a long drink of his margarita. "Okay. Let's not waste our time on him. We have something to tell you."

"Oh my gosh, what?"

"We think that by the end of the year or early next year we might be in the city as well."

"Really? You guys! That would be so great! I would love for you to move there."

"Well. We think . . . well . . . I think if we don't do it while we are single, we will never make the move."

I'm so thrilled to hear this. I would love my closest friends to live in the city.

"We would all have so much fun."

Heather plays with her hair. She seems a little nervous. "Moving there seems so overwhelming."

"Yes. Maybe at first. But you will get used to it quickly. Also, you will have me! I can help you! I would love to see you all the time in the city."

I love seeing my friends this evening and hearing the good news, but I am extra tired this evening, because of my late night before. We finish eating and end the night early. When I get to my parents' house, they are on the couch watching a movie, and I cozy up next to them. This wasn't the most exciting birthday I've ever had, but it was nice, and I am very happy.

Sunday morning, Dad makes a family breakfast before we head back to the city. David bought some groceries for us to drag back to the city, which is kind of a pain, but at least we would have some food for the week. I hug Mum goodbye and tell her I will see her soon. As I say goodbye Dad at the station, I ask him to meet for lunch downtown sometime soon. David and I once again drag all our stuff to train platform. Another weekend is almost over.

I'm at the Fullerton station on Monday morning waiting for the Red Line train when I notice a guy on the platform that I have seen a few times before. He looks over at me and smiles. Maybe he has noticed me, too, during the last few weeks? He is really cute. As the train pulls into the station, I make sure to get into the same car as him.

Once on the train, we are standing close together. Since the train is so crowded, we can't say anything to each other. He gets off at the Grand stop, which is one stop before mine. As I watch him get lost in the crowd, I wonder when I will see him again.

Over the next few days, he is on the train platform standing in the exact same spot. I'm pretty sure he is doing this on purpose. Thursday morning, he comes up next to me.

"It's funny how I keep seeing you."

I look up at him. "Yep, I've noticed you a few times too."

I can feel myself starting to blush, and I tell myself to be cool. We board our train and chat all the way to his stop at Grand.

"So, maybe I will see you tomorrow?"

"I hope so." I watch him as he disappears into the crowd just like he has done every day this week.

I walk briskly into work and tell James, Jillian, Amy, Kourtney, and Natalie that I finally talked to "Train Boy," a nickname we have been calling him all this week. I tell them what happened that morning. His name is Kevin.

James puts on his fake girly voice. "Oh, Kevin. So cute. I wonder if he will ask you on a date?"

I laugh, but I secretly hope he will. It has been a long time since I've been on a date.

"I don't know. Maybe."

"Well, I bet your "Chocolate Chip Cookie Guy" is going to be so jealous."

"Ugh, James! Please don't remind me!"

This week we signed a new client who lives in Indianapolis. I had an introductory call with him to go over his project, and he literally told me halfway through the call that I was his little chocolate chip cookie. It was so strange.

Over the last few days, he has been emailing me about his project non-stop. He tells me he is coming to Chicago soon. I really hope he doesn't. I looked him up on Facebook, and his pictures look normal but calling me his little chocolate chip cookie just weirds me out. Even if he never mentioned the chocolate chip cookie thing, I'm definitely not interested in someone who lives a few hours away.

When Vin walks in, James can't help but tell Vin about what happened with "train boy." Vin gives me a big grin.

"So, are you going to go on a date with him?"

"I don't know. Why?"

"I think your new friend is going to be jealous."

"Ha Ha, very funny. I don't want anything to do with him. I can't wait 'til we are done with this project so he will leave me alone."

"You know he wants to come to Chicago for a little visit."

"What! How do you know that? Did he actually tell you that?"

"Yep. He sure did." Vin laughs at me and walks back into his office.

I look over at James. He's laughing too. I shake my head and walk back to my desk.

Friday night is my city birthday dinner with Jillian, James, and now, Vin. I almost forgot about it. I call the restaurant, and luckily, I get a reservation for four at seven. I leave the office on Friday evening with a plan for us to all meet at the restaurant.

Just before seven, I pull up in a cab and walk into this quaint little restaurant. I have wanted to eat at a local spot since I moved here, and I'm so excited to try this place. When I think of city restaurants, this is what I imagine. Quaint, cozy, and lots of character.

James and Jillian are at a little table that doesn't seem like it will fit two more people. I greet them each with a hug and join them at our teeny table. Ten minutes later, Vin strolls in and heads toward us.

"Wow, this place looks great. Good choice, Kell." I give him a smile. The waiter places four glasses of water and fresh bread on our table, and I help myself to the bread.

"Thanks for coming. This table is a little small, but I think we will be okay."

We look over our menus in silence. The descriptions of the food sound so delicious. My mouth starts to water, and I'm starting to feel really hungry. We start with drinks and decide on a bottle of red wine for our table.

The waiter comes back with our bottle and four glasses. We are ready to order, and I order cheese ravioli. My favorite. The server takes our menus, and we all *cheers* as they wish me Happy Birthday.

I notice that Vin is quiet this evening. He is just listening to our conversation. I give him a few side-way glances, but he doesn't notice. I wonder why he is so preoccupied?

"So, you guys. We have to check out this new bar that's . . ."

"My girlfriend moved out last weekend." James stops mid-sentence, and the three of us look over at Vin.

I reach over and gently and touch his arm. "Oh no. What happened?"

"Well, I told you Kell, but ever since we moved in together, it just hasn't seemed right. We moved in because we thought it was the right next step, but I knew I didn't want to go any further with her. It was wrong of me to move in with her, and I felt bad, but I had to end it. We were both not happy. I gave her some money to help get her own place. She is currently staying with a friend right now."

"Wow. Vin. I'm so sorry to hear that. I knew you guys were not getting along, but I'm sorry it had to end that way."

"Yeah, me too. But, I know she is not the girl for me. I realized that once she moved in. I should have been more honest about how I felt before she moved in."

We sit in silence for what seems like a few minutes. I don't think anyone knew what to say or wants to start another conversation. The waiter ends the awkward silence as he fills our wine glasses.

The rest of the evening is great. We chat, enjoy our food, and have a few glasses of wine. The food is amazing, and the conversation is light-hearted and fun. We don't ask Vin any more questions. I am really enjoying all their company and, yes, even my boss. We have come a long way since that first interview, and I'm glad I have included him this evening. It's actually not that weird.

The three of them take care of the bill. I try to pay my share. It's sweet that they want to treat me, and I thank them for joining me to celebrate my birthday. James makes a few suggestions for other restaurants we should try, including a place called *Ann Sather* that has the best cinnamon rolls. It's not far from where we are now. As we leave for the evening, we make a plan to go there for brunch soon.

ELEVEN

I see "Train Boy" again on Monday morning, which instantly puts me in a good mood.

"Hey. I was wondering if I would run into you," he said. "How was your weekend?"

"It was good. Yours?"

"Same, good. Normal weekend. I was also wondering, do you have plans for this Thursday?"

"Umm. I don't think so. Why?"

"Well, I thought that maybe we could get a glass of wine and a small bite at this little wine bar in Lincoln Park."

"That sounds great. Oh, wait. I should probably give you my number."

We exchange numbers before the train arrives and continue talking the whole way to his stop at Grand.

"Have a good day. If I don't see you before, I'll see you Thursday."

As I walk into the office that morning, I feel like I'm on cloud nine.

"Well, someone is in a good mood for a Monday."

I sit down across from James at his desk. "Well, someone has a date with "Train Boy" on Thursday."

He stops typing on his computer and looks at me. "Ooooh seriously? That's great! Good for you!"

"I really need to stop calling him "Train Boy." Knowing me, I will probably say that to his face."

"Yes, you probably will."

I roll my eyes at him. "Okay. Well, I just wanted to let you know the good news. We can chat more about it later."

I walk to my desk, sit down, and take a big sip of my coffee. All I can think about is how I can't wait for Thursday.

I check my email and see one with the subject line, "My Little Chocolate Chip Cookie." Oh no! What could he want now? I open the email and skim through. My stomach is instantly in knots. He's coming to Chicago on March 29th for the night, and he wants to go to dinner. I can't believe it! I don't want to have dinner with him.

What do I do? How do I respond? He is a client after all. I feel it would be rude to turn him down. I send an instant message to James.

OMG! GUESS WHAT! Chocolate Chip Cookie Guy is coming here on March 29th, and he wants to go to dinner!

He responds with about ten laughing faces.

James! I'm serious! What should I do?

I think you just have to suck it up and go to dinner. Kelly, just make sure he knows it's a business dinner or something. Say that you can go over some project details or something.

Why do I even have to go?

Ya don't. But he's an important client right now, and with you talking to him so much, you have led him on a little. Don't you think?

Maybe. But I wasn't trying to do that. I was just being nice.

What did I get myself into! Later that day, I tell Vin what happened with "Chocolate Chip Cookie Guy." He just starts laughing.

"I'm really sorry, but it's kind of your fault. You have been so nice to him. You keep responding to all his emails."

"I know! But I'm nice. I'm just nice. I can't be mean. I thought I was being friendly and doing my job."

Toward the end of the day, I respond to "Chocolate Chip Cookie Guy" and tell him that I can do dinner, but I have plans later in the evening. I tell him we can go over some project details, like James suggested, and try to make my email sound as professional as possible. He responds right back with a smiley face and tells me he can't wait. Oh boy! What on earth did I get myself into!

I'm sitting in my room on Thursday evening trying to figure out what to wear for my big date. Gracie is hanging out with me exploring my bedroom. My brother is not home, so I can't ask him. I feel like I haven't seen David much. He has been working weird hours lately. I don't even know if he knows I'm going on my date tonight.

I finally decide to wear a sleeveless top, jeans, heels, and my leather jacket. Spring is almost here in Chicago, so it's not as freezing anymore. It's nice not having to wear a sweater and a heavy coat. I'm going from cab to the bar and home again, so I don't need to be all bundled up. I check my makeup and hair, and I look at my phone. James has sent me a good luck text with a wink face. I respond back with a smiley face as I hear footsteps coming up the stairs.

The apartment door opens, and David walks in. I run into the living room to greet him. He has a big smile on his face.

"Good day?"

"Yeah, it was. I had lunch with one of the directors of the hotel, and he is really impressed with all my hard work and said that next month I can move up to the gym."

"Oh my gosh! That's so exciting! Congratulations! I'm so proud of you!"

"Thank you! I'm excited about it. You will have to come by and try the gym or one of the classes."

"Oh, I definitely will. I'm sure it's nice. You know . . . I would love to chat more about your job, but I have to leave. I have a date tonight."

"Oh, with who?"

"You remember "Train Boy" I was telling you about? Him."

"Really? You actually talked to him."

"Yep. We chatted a bit last week and then on Monday he asked me to go out. We are meeting at a wine bar in Lincoln Park."

"Wow. Well, have a good time then."

"I will! If you are still up when I get home, I will tell you all about it. We can also chat more about your job."

"Maybe. But I probably won't be. I have to be at work early again, but we can talk soon."

"Okay, let's do that. I feel like we haven't really seen much of each other lately."

I give David a huge long hug. I really do miss him. I grab my leather jacket and my bag, slide into my heels, and head out the front door.

As always when it's dark out, I walk down the middle of the street, as quickly as I can, in my heels and up to Sheffield to catch a cab. I know I must look like an idiot, but I don't care. I don't think I will ever get used to walking in the dark alone. A cab comes along, I get in, and tell him where I'm going. I haven't been to this area much since dating Dylan. It's such an adorable area with little boutiques and restaurants.

Less than ten minutes later, I get out of the cab and head into this quaint little wine bar. Low lighting makes the bar look cozy. There are pretty couches, comfy chairs, and coffee tables. There is a lit tea light candle in the middle of each table. I spot Kevin toward the back of the bar, and he's sitting in one of two oversized chairs.

He stands up to greet me with a quick hug.

"Hi! This place is adorable! Have you ever been here before?" I sit down in the other oversized chair across from him.

"No. But my roommate has, and he said it is a good place to come for wine. I guess they have a great wine selection."

"I can see that." I quickly glance over the menu.

We take a few minutes to look over all the choices. We choose a few small plates and two glasses of red wine. It seems as though many restaurants in the city are all about small plates and sharing. I like the idea of it, but I'm not used to choosing what to eat with others, especially with someone I don't know. I guess it makes dining more intimate and gives you the option to try more things on the menu.

We enjoy our wine and our small plates and chat about the typical things you talk about on a first date. Where we work. Where we went to school. Where we live. It's a friendly conversation but not great. I don't feel like I have found my soulmate. It almost feels like I'm being interviewed. As we finish our wine, he looks over at me.

"So, how old are you?"

"Huh?"

"I'm just wondering. It seems like you have been out of college a little longer than me. You worked in the 'burbs at a preschool before moving here."

I'm not ashamed of telling him my age. I'm still young. I'm in my twenties. However, our conversation didn't seem to flow right all night. I feel like I'm being judged.

"I'm twenty-six."

"Oh. Really? Do you know how old I am?"

"I don't know. I figure around the same as me."

"I'm twenty-two."

"Okay." I didn't know what else he wanted me to say and, suddenly, the vibe between us has changed.

We sit there for a second. I didn't know how to continue the conversation. Did I really want to date a twenty-two-year-old? Probably not.

"I think that maybe, maybe umm, you probably want something a little more serious than what I'm looking for. I just moved here from college."

"Yep. Okay. I totally get it. I'm not looking to get married tomorrow or anything, but I get what you are saying."

The whole conversation has become strange, and I don't feel like engaging anymore. The server comes by, and Kevin asks for the bill. It's nice of him to pay, and he should since he just made the night totally awkward. We stand up to leave and put on our coats.

"Kelly, I do think you're really nice. We can still chat on the train, right, and be friends?"

"Yeah, of course! Totally." I'm so ready to go home. He keeps making this evening more awkward by the minute.

I walk out of the bar and, thank goodness, a cab has pulled over, and I get in.

"Okay, see you on the train! Thank you for the wine and food."

"Yep. Good night!"

As the cab heads down Halsted, I pull out my phone to text James. It's only 10:03, and he's probably still up.

He's 22.

Oh, really? No good, you don't want to date a kid. Next. Tell me more about it tomorrow. Night.

I take a deep breath, sigh, put my phone back in my bag and look out the window. Oh well. It's for the best. I was a little bummed since I was so excited to go on this date. Kevin seemed so great. Well, maybe "Chocolate Chip Cookie Guy" will be better. I giggle to myself because I seriously doubt it from his corny emails.

The next morning at the Fullerton platform, I'm a little nervous to see Kevin. I look around at all the people waiting for the train, but I don't see him at all. The train pulls into the station. I get on and the doors shut. No more "Train Boy."

TWELVE

I walk into work and, of course, the first thing I do is tell the girls about my date with "Train Boy."

"Kelly, you should know that once we get to our age, you want to make sure you only date a guy who is mature and established, and someone knows what he wants in life. So, you definitely don't want to date a twenty-two-year-old. An older guy is always the way to go."

"Yep. You're so right, Kourtney."

I thought she is somewhat right. Older, yes. Established? I don't need a guy who already knows everything he wants. I want someone who is my best friend, someone who likes the same things as me. The rest we can figure out together.

However, I listen as she keeps going one.

"You know, younger guys are like children, and they just play games. You should always find out his age first and, especially, what they do for a career. You want to make sure he can take care of you. My fiancé is in finance, so I knew he would be able to take care of me. He was just right from the beginning. He . . . "

"Oh, can you hold that thought for a second. I think I hear my desk phone."

"Oh. Sure. I will be right here. Always happy to give more advice." She flashes me a smile, and I walk out of the room.

My desk phone stops ringing, but I see my instant messenger is flashing, and it's James.

Do you want to go to this spot called Mercadito after work? I hear they have the best margaritas in the city.

Yes! Perfect! Just what I need!

As the day continues, I just can't shake my bad mood, although I try. I am not looking forward to my date tomorrow night with "Chocolate Chip Cookie Guy." I have a working lunch with Vin today, but we talk mostly about how his ex-girlfriend keeps calling. She is trying to make him feel bad, and it's getting him down. I am also in a bad mood about tomorrow night, I tell him.

"Oh, yeah. Your big date tomorrow."

"Stop calling it a date but yep. I feel like I have to go because he is driving all the way here. James said I made him feel as though I'm interested. But, I'm not. Since he is a client, I'm going to go."

"Well, you never know until you go. He might just be your dream guy."

I roll my eyes at him and take a bite of my salad.

"You know what?"

"What?"

"I'm going to pick you up and drive you tomorrow night. I kind of feel responsible for this "date" since he is a client. You are totally put on the spot. I want to make sure that he's not crazy. I don't want to lose my best assistant."

"Ha. Ha. Thank you for that, but you really don't have to. I will be okay. We are meeting at *Cafe Ba-Ba-Reeba!*"

"No. I'm picking you up. If you don't feel comfortable, call me, and I will come get you."

"Really?"

"Really."

"Okay, thanks. That is so nice of you."

"Of course. What time do you have to be there?"

"Seven."

"Okay. I'll be by your house around six forty-five. Just text me your address tomorrow."

"Okay, I will. Oh, by the way, James said we could all meet at *Ann Sather* on Sunday. Do you want to come? I think I'm going to invite my brother as well. He doesn't really know anyone in the city."

"Okay, yeah. I'll come."

"Good. I can't wait to try those cinnamon rolls.

James and I make it to *Mercadito* just in time for happy hour. We both order a regular margarita with spicy salt, mango guacamole, and a variety of tacos. James is right about the margaritas. They are strong and delicious. I drink the first one too quickly, and I'm feeling really tipsy after the second.

Halfway through our meal, I look around *Mercadito*. It is packed, and the vibe is fun. I like this place. Most of the night, we chat about dating and wonder why guys are always so strange. We share a lot of funny dating stories, which are funnier after a few drinks. My stomach is literally hurting by the end of the night. I start feeling better about tomorrow night. Well, maybe just a little.

I hang around my apartment all day on Saturday just waiting for tonight. I am not hungover from the margaritas last night, but I spend the day doing nothing. I feel a tad sorry for myself because I have to go on this date tonight, although I know there are way worst things in life. I catch up on the Real Housewives of Beverly Hills and, as I'm watching TV, I receive a few emails from "Chocolate Chip Cookie Guy." He is excited to come to Chicago and go out to dinner.

He says he will be at his hotel around four and I can meet him there for a drink before dinner. I tell him I cannot meet before, but I am looking forward to tonight. I feel so guilty for lying. I try to make my email responses sound cheery as I can. I feel like a horrible person, but I seriously have no interest in dating someone from another state. I should have been honest with him from the beginning, then he wouldn't be coming all the way here.

I text my address to Vin and ask him if he still wants to drive me tonight. He will be there, he says. It's forty-five minutes before he is supposed to pick me up, and I'm slowly starting to get ready. I put on a light sweater, jeans, and my new favorite cognac boots. Nothing fancy, just something I typically wear when I go out to dinner with the girls. I lay on my bed and wait for the text from Vin. I tell myself that I am only going out for a few hours. It will be over soon. I can definitely get through this one dinner.

At six forty-five Vin sends me a text that's he's outside. I grab my stuff and head out to meet him. I see a black car and assume it's his. It's a beautiful BMW X5, and I tell him that as soon as I open the door and get in.

"Oh, yeah this thing? I got it a few months ago. I've always wanted one." He is grinning, and I can tell he is proud of his new car.

"Maybe I can drive it sometime?"

"Nah." I look over at him, and he gives me another grin.

We start driving in the direction of the restaurant. I give a big sigh and lay back in the passenger seat.

"You really don't want to go, do you?"

"No, I don't, and I feel so bad about all of this."

"You should! The guy came all the way here for nothing. You have totally led him on."

"I know! I'm such a terrible person, right?"

"No. You just have to start being more honest with people. It's okay to say no. You didn't have to chat with him through emails. You should have kept it professional. That's what you really should have done."

"Yeah, you are so right. I'm so sorry. I wasn't professional at all. I didn't even think about that. I was just friendly. I really should have been honest and kept it professional from the beginning."

"Well, don't be too hard on yourself. He should have been more professional as well. But, just go, try to enjoy, and text me if you need anything."

We are nearing *Cafe Ba-Ba-Reeba!* on Halsted, and Vin slows down the car to a stop.

"Let me know how it goes. I'll pull over and wait for a few minutes. You can text me that you are okay."

"Okay. Thank you so much for driving me."

"No problem."

I take a deep breath and open the door to the restaurant. It's packed inside, and I recognize him from his Facebook picture, as he's looking around anxiously. Alright, it's just one dinner, and it's just for a few hours. He spots me walking toward him, grins from ear to ear, and puts out his arms.

"My little Chocolate Chip Cookie! It's so nice to finally meet you."

"You too!" I give him a big smile and try to sound happy to meet him.

"Should we go to the bar and have a drink while we wait for our table?"

"Sure!"

I follow behind him and quickly pull out my phone to text Vin. *I'm okay.* We look around for a seat and spot two people getting up from the bar. We head toward them and grab the two stools. I put my jacket over my bar stool and settle in. The bartender hands us two menus, and I take a few minutes to look over the drink list.

"You know, I've never been here before. I've heard the food is good. It's a popular restaurant."

"I'll say! It's packed in here. I'm surprised we got a seat at the bar."

"Yep." I read the menu to choose what I want to drink. I decide on a glass of red sangria.

I catch eyes with the bartender, and he asks what we would like to drink. I tell him I want the red sangria and "Chocolate Chip Cookie Guy" orders the same. We chat while we wait for our drinks. Our conversation is a little awkward. We both don't know what to say. The bartender comes back with our sangrias and asks if we would like any food.

"Umm, actually, yes we would!"

I smile at the bartender and turn my seat to face "Chocolate Chip Cookie Guy." "You know, let's just eat at the bar since we are already here."

"Okay, if you really want to. I will cancel our table. I'll be right back."

"Okay great! Thanks!"

He gets up and heads over to the host stand. We will probably have to wait at least another twenty minutes for our table. I know I'm a terrible person but the vibe between us is so uncomfortable. He comes back, and we order some tapas. We sip on our sangria and wait for our food. There is a lot of awkward silence, and we mostly talk about what's going on around us.

We don't have to wait too long for our food. This date is not going well, but the food is delicious. I love the Brussels sprouts salad. I need to come here again. I'll have to ask the girls if they want to do a girl's night here. Maybe next week. They have a happy hour. I snap myself back to reality and try to focus on our conversation. Am I the only person on the planet who has ever done something like this because I just feel so awful. I can't get into this dinner, and my mind again continues to wander.

"Hey, is everything is okay?"

"Oh. Yeah. I'm fine. Sorry, I'm suddenly feeling a little tired. Must have been the sangria."

"Would you like anything else?"

"No. I mean, no thanks, I'm full. Everything was so tasty though." I give him a reassuring smile.

"Okay, me too. So, where to next? What time are your other plans tonight? Not 'til later right?"

I look at him and just stare. What? Oh no! Other plans? I completely forgot I told him that. I glance at my phone, and I see that it's only 7:43 pm. We haven't even been here for an hour. Oh geez! This guy came all the way here, and I'm only going to spend less than an hour with him. Of course, he wants to go somewhere else.

"Hmm. I'm not sure. I'm going to go to the bathroom really quick. I will be right back."

"Okay. I will be right here."

I don't know what to do. How am I going to get out of this? I look at my text messages, and I see a response from Vin.

How's it going?

We are done eating, and he now wants to go somewhere else.

You are done eating already?

Yep. We ate at the bar. The conversation is really awkward. I don't want to go somewhere else, but it's only been 45 minutes.

Just tell him you don't feel well. I'm leaving right now to come get you. Be there in 10.

Really?

Yep.

Okay.

I can't believe Vin is coming to get me. For a second, it makes me feel good, and I relax a bit. But, then, I feel nervous again. What am I going to tell him? How am I going to get out of here that quickly? I have never done anything like this before, and now I'm nervous. I never wanted to purposely hurt someone's feelings. This is definitely a lesson learned, and I will never do anything like this to someone again. I walk back to the bar and hop back onto my bar stool.

"So. What should we do? What do you like to do in the city?"

"I'm so sorry. I think something didn't sit well with me. I'm going to have to go home."

His face drops. "Really? Well, we could go back to your place and just relax."

"Oh, I don't think that's a good idea. I'm feeling worse every minute. I'm going to have to cancel my other plans as well."

"Oh, okay." He looks really hurt, and I feel terrible.

"Here. Let me get this." I signal for the bar tab. "It's my treat. I feel terrible, especially since you came all the way here."

He shrugs his shoulders as I hand my credit card to the bartender. I can tell he is upset, especially since he didn't object to me paying for our meal. I deserve to pay since I was so misleading to this poor guy. I sign the check, and we get up to leave. A couple asks if they can have our stools, and I tell them yes. The fact that they seem happy to be out with each other makes me feel even more guilty. We walk out of the restaurant, and he sees a bar all lit up across the street.

"I think I will just go over there."

"Okay. I'm so sorry."

He nods at me, turns away, and starts walking in the direction of the bar. I hear my phone beep, and I see a text from Vin that he is here. I watch until "Chocolate Chip Cookie Guy" is out of sight, and I look around for Vin's BMW. I see him parked a few buildings down to my left. As I walk closer, he gets out of the car.

"Wow! That was the quickest dinner ever! I was barely home before you text me back."

"What are you doing? Why are you getting out of the car?"

"I'm letting you drive."

"What? No. I can't! You said no before."

"Well, I trust you."

"Really?"

"Really."

I give Vin a big smile and walk quickly to the driver's side and get in. I buckle my seatbelt and grab the steering wheel. Vin gets comfortable in the passenger seat.

I look over at him. "So, where should we go?"

"Wherever you want. Just drive and tell me about your worst date ever."

"It was not a date. But, okay." I pull out onto Halsted and head toward downtown.

We spend the next hour driving around the city. I tell him about my dinner, and then we just talk about anything. Music, movies, places we want to visit. Talking with Vin is easy, unlike my dinner conversation this evening, and we laugh a lot together. Why can't the guys I meet be more like Vin?

A little later, we are driving down Lake Shore Drive toward my house. I ask him what he thinks of Natalie. I don't know why I ask him. The question came out of nowhere, and I say it before I can stop myself. But, honestly, I am really curious.

"Okay, where did that question come from? She's nice. But we are just friends. She has asked me to hang out a few times."

"Are you going to hang out with her?"

"I don't know. We keep meaning to, but I haven't really thought much about it."

"Oh, okay. I was just wondering."

He looks over at me and gives me a strange look. He starts to say something, but I cut him off and quickly change the conversation.

"So, are you still coming to brunch tomorrow?"

"Yeah, if you guys are still going."

"We are. I think we are going around eleven."

"Cool. I'll be there."

"Okay. Hey, thanks so much for driving me, picking me up, and letting me drive your car. It was fun. I should be heading home. It's still early, but I was out last night at *Mercadito* and had a few margaritas. I've been feeling tired all day. Have you been there? The drinks are great."

"Yeah, I've been there. Those drinks are pretty strong."

"Yeah, they sure are and, you know, every time I go out with James it becomes a long night."

A few minutes later we pull onto my street, and I park the car in front of my apartment. I take off my seatbelt and turn to look at Vin.

"So, thanks again for everything tonight. It was fun, and I'll see you tomorrow?"

"Yep, of course. No problem. I'll see you tomorrow."

I get out of the car and walk down the path to my front door. I turn around and watch him drive away. I let out a sigh. He did save me tonight. He's really becoming a good friend. Other than James, I don't know who else I would have called to help me out. I walk into my apartment and see that David is in his bedroom.

"Hey, you're home early."

"Yeah. I'm tired, and I didn't want to hang out with that guy."

"That terrible? Two dates in a row."

"It wasn't really a date, but yeah. It was just awkward. I told you about "Chocolate Chip Cookie Guy.""

"Yep. You get yourself into some weird situations."

"Well, Vin picked me up early from my date, and we drove around for a bit. He let me drive his new car."

"Your boss picked you up and let you drive around in his car? That's weird."

"It's not like that. We are all friends in the office. He's also coming tomorrow to brunch. I'm excited for you to meet him and James. Jillian can't make it, because she already has brunch plans. But you can meet her another time."

"Well, it's still weird, but I'm looking forward to doing something tomorrow. I heard *Ann Sather* is good."

"I know! You haven't really done anything here, you just work so much or go home. I really think you will like my friends."

"I'm sure I will."

Well, I'm going to get in my pajamas. Let's watch some of *The Office* and catch up for a bit. The "Dinner Party" episode the other night was so funny. It's probably one of my favorites."

"Okay. Yeah, it was too funny."

THIRTEEN

David and I leave just before eleven to walk to *Ann Sather* for brunch. It's finally a beautiful, sunny day, and it will be a pretty walk to the restaurant. The fresh air will feel good. *Ann Sather* is not far, just up Sheffield to Belmont, and the restaurant is about a block down on the right.

"It's so nice to be outside and not be freezing cold. I'm looking forward to walking around the next few months and finally have the chance to explore more of the city."

"Yeah, it's nice. I actually walked all the way home from downtown the other day."

"Wow! You did? All the way from the Palmer House? That seems so far."

"It's a few miles, but it's a nice walk through Downtown, the Gold Coast, and Lincoln Park."

"How is work by the way?"

"It's good. I like it."

"What about the city? You don't seem to do much here other than work. You go home most weekends."

"I just don't really know anyone. I work weird hours, and I don't have time to do much else. I will probably stay for the rest of the year and see what happens after that."

My chest tightens up as he tells me this, but I know that it's true. He doesn't seem that happy here. He's not going out or doing anything fun. That's why I want him to come with me today. I want him to meet my friends and have some fun.

I can't worry about next January. It is months away and maybe he will love working at the health club and will want to stay. Who knows what I will be doing, and where I will be with my job in January. I know can't live with my brother forever, but I can't afford to live by myself right now, and I'm not moving home. I'm starting to love my life in the city way too much. As we walk into *Ann Sather,* I smell the freshly baked cinnamon rolls, and my mouth starts to water.

"Yum! Those rolls smell so good."

"Yeah they do, and this seems to be a popular place."

We arrive at *Ann Sather,* and it is super crowded. We squirm our way through the waiting customers and up to the counter. The hostess looks frazzled, but I ask her anyway if a James is waiting for us here. She doesn't say anything, grabs two menus, and motions for us to follow her. We walk into a second room and James is at a table in the middle of the restaurant.

"Hey, guys! I got here a little earlier to grab us a spot. It gets really busy here."

"I see that. James, this is my brother David. David, this is James."

The two shake hands and say hello. A guy comes over right away with glasses of water and asks if we want coffee. My brother and I say yes and within a minute we each have a mug in front of us filled with steaming hot coffee.

"Okay guys let me tell you about *Ann Sather* since you haven't been here before. You can order almost anything on the menu, and it comes with two sides. Everyone orders the cinnamon rolls and the potatoes as their sides."

I look at the tables around us. The portions are enormous, and the cinnamon rolls look like they could be a meal by themselves. It all looks so good. Vin joins us a few minutes later, and within a minute he also has a mug of hot coffee. James quickly again explains the menu to Vin.

"So, Kelly. I'm not sure if you've noticed this, but brunch is kind of a thing that everyone does in the city."

"This is actually my first brunch experience in the city."

"Really? Okay, well good. This will be a good one."

We each tell our server how we want our eggs cooked. I ask for over-easy and go with James' suggestion of the cinnamon rolls and potatoes. Minutes later, the server carries a large tray to our table with four enormous cinnamon rolls the size of my hand.

"Wait! We each get one of those?"

"Yep!"

Each order comes with two rolls spackled in thick icing. They smell ridiculously good. The same server fills our coffee mugs, and we dig in. I take a deep bite into the roll as the warm gooey icing dribbles onto my chin. Oh my gosh! It's heavenly. I end up eating most of the cinnamon rolls, and I can't believe I have more food coming. I definitely can't eat like this all the time.

Our food arrives, and it's excellent, but we all agree that the cinnamon rolls are the bomb and a must-have. We finish what we can of our meal and ask for more coffee. Our plates are cleared, and the four of us sit around chatting about anything and everything as we enjoy the rest of our coffees. I'm overjoyed to see that David seems to be having a fun time. My new friends are very welcoming, and I can tell they are enjoying his company as well.

As the men are talking, I look around the restaurant and see that it is not as crowded as before. There are still a few people sitting around with their coffee, but most of the tables around us are empty. I check my phone. It is almost two-thirty.

"You guys, we have been here for a while." The three of them check their phones.

"We have to make sure to give our server a good tip. We have taken up his table for a long time." As soon as I say this, our server comes over and offers us more coffee.

"Would you guys like more coffee or anything else? I just want to let you know we are closing soon."

"No. We are good. Sorry for sitting for so long and taking up your table."

"It's no problem. I don't mind."

"Okay, thank you. You can bring the check whenever."

"I actually have it right here."

We each pay what we owe and get up to leave. "Okay, guys, I will see you in the morning. Thanks for a fun first brunch experience. Everything was delicious, but next time, I probably only need to get the cinnamon rolls. I'm so full."

"I'm glad you enjoyed, it is a lot of food. Okay, you guys enjoy the rest of your Sunday and see you tomorrow Kell."

"You too. Bye, James." I look over at David. "You ready to walk back home?"

"Yep, let's go." As we walk down Belmont, I ask him what he thought of Vin and James.

"They are both really nice. It was fun, and I'm glad I came."

I link arms with my brother and look up to give him a wide smile. "Good. I'm glad. I'm so happy you came with me."

FOURTEEN

I have to say that there's something that happens here in Chicago during the springtime. It's only the beginning of April, but something truly magical starts to happen in the city. The trees and flowers come into bloom. One of the prettiest and well-known attractions is the beds of tulips, thousands of them, in varieties of colors that come to life along Michigan Avenue. It's a sight to behold after the long cold months of Chicago's winters. You can feel the city literally coming back to life.

The city people have a little more bounce in their step. Strangers look up at you with a smile instead of down, heads buried between their shoulders, their gaze toward the ground. Happy chatter is all around. It's the time of the year that instantly warms you inside, and you realize why you choose to live in this city.

Chicagoans live for the spring and summer. They make the most of every moment, and for a good reason. The winters here are tough. I will follow all the girls' advice and promise myself that next year, I will be prepared with the right boots, clothes, and a warmer coat. I have to say that once the weather changes you sort of forget about the last few blustery months and just how cold it truly was. I love summer so much! I'm very excited for my first spring and summer here in the city.

I check my email on Monday. Nothing from "Chocolate Chip Cookie Guy." I feel relieved but also a little sad. I'm sure I hurt his feelings, and that wasn't my intention. I go back and forth in my head about whether I should email him. I decide to email him to make sure he got back to Indianapolis okay. I ask if he enjoyed Chicago. He responds right away. He liked the city. He ended up hanging with a few people from the bar for the rest of the night, and he hoped I was feeling better. Yes, I'm much better, I tell him, and I'm glad he enjoyed the rest of his night. Okay, I now feel relieved. At least he wasn't stuck being alone.

The temperature is a high of fifty-seven degrees and sunny, so most of the office is leaving for lunch. Everyone wants to enjoy a warmer, sunny day. I'm at my desk thinking about what to do for lunch. I want to find out where everyone is going when I feel someone standing next to me. I look up, and it's Vin.

"You want to go for a walk and get lunch today? We could talk about some more projects that I might have for you."

I really don't want to talk about work. I want to just get outside and enjoy the fresh air and sunshine.

"Yep, okay."

"Well, grab your stuff and let's go. I really need to get some air."

"Okay. I'm coming."

We walk out onto Michigan Avenue. I'm greeted with sunshine on my face rather than a blast of cold air. Oh, it feels lovely to be outside. The buildings are gleaming from the sun, and the Chicago River has a brilliant sparkle. It's especially busy at this time of day. People all along the Avenue are wearing their coats open and smiles on their faces. They're making the most of this beautiful day. We start walking without saying much. We are not in a rush, so we walk for a little bit longer.

"So, what new projects do you have for me."

"Well, I was wondering if you would be interested in taking over all the billing and invoicing for the office. You are really organized, and it would be a huge help. James and I really don't have time anymore."

"Well, I don't know too much about accounting, but I'm willing to learn and take on the challenge."

"Good. James can go over the basics with you, and I have no doubt you can figure out the rest."

This is a great opportunity. My role in the office is continuing to change. I've been putting in a lot of hard work and dedication, and it's starting to pay off. I'm hoping to get a little raise after taking on so much more work. I will wait to see how everything goes with my new responsibilities.

"Okay, I feel like we've gotten some fresh air. Are you ready to go eat?"

"Yep. I'm getting pretty hungry."

"Okay, we're close to this restaurant called *Beatrix*. Have you heard of it?"

"No. I hardly know any restaurants. I've been making a list of all the restaurants I come across and want to try."

"You'll like it. I met a client there, and both the coffee and food are really good."

"Okay great. Let's go."

We walk around the corner, and I see the sign for *Beatrix*. The restaurant is at the Aloft Hotel. I love a trendy hotel restaurant or bar so I will enjoy this place. *Beatrix* is not busy, and we are able to get a table right away. The host seats us at a cozy little table with two oversized chairs. I love the decor of *Beatrix*, it has a warm atmosphere. They have a cute coffee bar filled with delicious pastries and desserts. We both order right away. I ask for the Straight A Salad. Vin gets a turkey burger. Our food doesn't take long, and once it arrives I'm starving, so I dive right in.

"I know we talked the other night about our favorite '80s movies. But have you seen any good movies at the theater lately?"

"Actually, no I haven't. I love going to the movies, but right now I don't have anyone to go with me, and I don't like going alone."

"Well, I don't really have anyone to go with me either, and if you want, we could go see a movie?" I look up from my salad and give him a surprised look.

"Oh, sorry if that threw you off. I just thought we could go as friends. Since we both like movies, I just thought it would be an idea."

I did like the idea, and I love movies. Vin and I did get along well so it would be nice to see a movie. Is it strange to go to a movie with your boss? I wasn't sure. But I respond before I can think about it too much.

"Oh, yeah, totally, I would love that."

"Okay. Maybe let's go next week?"

"Yeah, I'm free."

"Cool. You ready to head back to the office. We have been gone a while."

"Yep, I'm ready." I take one last sip from my latte, and we head back to work.

The following week, I'm totally swamped with work. I'm learning all I can about QuickBooks and figuring out all the billing. I hate to admit to Vin that things are not that organized. I know the team, especially James, is happy to have the invoices organized for their clients. I've been working with both Vin and James to come up with a system to get things paid and how to send invoices. I enjoy being a big part of the team. I'm so much more involved in the day to day.

This evening, Vin and I are going to see a movie. He will pick me up and drive me home. He lives downtown. I tell him he doesn't need to do that since the theater is downtown. But he insists that it's not a big deal. I haven't told anyone about the movie, except for James. I really don't want to make it a big thing, because it's not, but people like to talk. I especially don't want Natalie to know I'm going with him. She is still trying to get him to hang out with her.

It's just before seven, and I'm ready to go. I get a text from Vin.

Here.

Okay, coming out in 2 seconds.

K.

I get into his black SUV. "Thanks for picking me up. You really didn't have to."

"It's no problem, it's not far for me."

Fifteen minutes later, we pull into the theater's parking garage, which is just off Michigan Avenue. We head inside and up two huge escalators. Vin tells the girl at the ticket counter that we would like two tickets.

"Vin! You can't drive and then also pay for my ticket. I can pay."

"I got it." He hands the girl his credit card.

"Okay, well thank you. That is really nice. I'm going to buy us some popcorn then." We get our snacks and head into our theater.

"Do you care where we sit?"

"No. Anywhere is fine."

"Okay. Up here. I like sitting in the way back. I don't like anyone sitting behind me."

"Okay. That's fine." I follow him up the theater stairs and sit down next to him.

As I watch the previews, I start to feel a little nervous and awkward that Vin is sitting right next to me at a movie. My boss is at a movie with me and just paid for my ticket. I feel like I'm doing something wrong. But, on the other hand, it's also strange because I feel comfortable around him. He feels like an old friend, and we find it easy to hang out and talk to each other. I have not felt this way with the last few guys I have met.

"You okay?"

"Yep, I'm good."

"That last preview looked really good. I love anything with The Rock in it."

"Yeah, I like him too."

"I'll watch most movies though, as long as they look good."

"Oh, me too." The lights dim down signaling the start of the movie. The credits start playing, and I grab a handful of popcorn and settle into my seat.

Before I know it, it's an hour and a half later, and we slowly walk back down the steps and out of the theater.

"What did you think of the movie? I thought the writing was good."

"It was great. I love a good drama. It's a good sign when you can talk about the movie afterward."

"I agree. We can discuss the movie in the car if you want. I like to do that too. Since we both like movies so much, we have to go see another movie again soon."

"For sure."

Vin drops me off at my apartment. I walk in and see the light on in my brother's room. I lightly knock. "Come in!"

I slowly open the door and walk in. "How was the movie? Who did you go with? James?"

"No, actually I went with Vin."

"Wait! No, you didn't! I know you guys hang out with James, but now you are going to the movies with him alone?"

"No, it's not what you think. We are just friends. We both love seeing movies. We talked about how we don't have friends who like going to movies as much as we do. So, we decided to go."

"Okay. Well just be careful. That could really affect things at your job."

"I know. It's not an all the time thing. Trust me. I like my job too much to ruin things, and I have no interest in dating my boss. That would just be weird."

"Okay, whatever you say."

"It's fine. Well, I'm going to bed. It's getting late."

"Okay, good night."

"Night."

As I walk toward my room, I have that weird feeling again that I'm doing something wrong. I try to push the feeling aside and get ready for bed. I call for Gracie, so she will come lay with me. I guess I should take a step back from him. If my brother doesn't think it's a good idea, and I don't want people to know, it's probably not a good thing. I really don't want anyone to get the wrong idea about us.

FIFTEEN

I spend the next week or so completely engrossed in my work.
I'm busy every day and hardly have time to chat with either
the team or the girls like I used to. However, today I'm taking
a break to have lunch at the sushi place with Jillian. It is nice to have
girl time. I'm about to take a bite of my spicy tuna roll when Jillian
almost makes me jump.

"Oh! I can't believe it. I forgot to tell you. A few events are
coming up that seem really fun. The spring events are way better
because everyone wants to come out of hibernation. I know I've
promised to take you with me to an event. Next week we can go to
one that I think you will really like."

"Really? I can really go?"

"Yep. I can put your name on the list, and we can go
from work."

"Oh yay! I'm so excited! Thank you for inviting me."

"Yeah, no problem."

I don't think she understands just how excited I am. This is my
first official fashion event, and I was invited. Me! Someone who
hardly knows anything about the city. I couldn't believe it! I must
make sure I have something really cool and trendy to wear.

I call my Mum after work to fill her in on everything I have been up to. I chat about my new responsibilities at work, what I've been up to with my friends and my invite to the fashion event. I didn't tell her about going to the movies with Vin. I'm not sure if she would approve either. She would just be worried that it might affect my job, as well.

For my first fashion event, I decide to wear a blue blazer, jeans, and my favorite pair of strappy heel sandals. Hopefully, my outfit is trendy enough to make a good impression. Jillian and I head to the event straight from work, which is at Kenneth Cole on Michigan Avenue. Jillian tells me the event is to promote his new shoe collection and there's a chance Kenneth Cole might be there. I guess in larger markets like Chicago, he likes to be present to promote his own shoes. I don't know much about Kenneth Cole or his shoes, but it would be cool to meet a designer.

I notice that some of the team is heading out for the evening, so I shut down my computer and walk over to Jillian. I'm starting to feel a little anxious about this evening because I've never been around press or the essential people who cover these events. I'm anticipating all the things that could happen because I just don't know what to expect. Jillian is still busy tapping away on her computer, but she looks up and smiles at me as I sit down next to her.

"What are you working on?"

"Just getting ahead on some blog posts and social media for clients this month. We are looking to hire a few more people to help with all the work. That will help me a lot. I can't seem to keep up these days. I'm working such long hours right now."

"Oh, that will be great if you can hire some help. You don't want to get burnt out."

"No, I really don't." She closes her laptop and folds her arms on top of it.

"So about tonight. You can just stay with me if you want. I have to make the rounds and take some photos. After that, we can just hang out."

"Okay, that's good. I can for sure just follow your lead. I'm so looking forward to it."

I'm not going to tell her how nervous I am. We get ready to leave, and I walk around the office to make sure everything is turned off. I notice that Vin is still working.

"Hey Kell, what are you still doing here?"

"Oh, Jillian and I are going to an event. She invited me to go with her."

"Cool. Have fun."

"Yeah, I will. See you tomorrow." I give him a slight wave that he doesn't see. He is typing again on this computer.

We walk toward Kenneth Cole, and I'm probably driving Jillian nuts with questions about what happens at these events.

"Usually it's a mix of press, Chicago influencers or bloggers, and bigger websites like the one I work for. After you have been to a few, you will recognize a lot of the same people. Each event varies in size, and the size also depends on how much hype or promotion the store does. This one seems to have a lot more hype."

"Wow, it sounds like this could be a big deal."

"This one might be because of the brand, especially if Kenneth Cole actually comes. I told you I wanted to bring you to the best one."

"Yep, you did."

I'm thinking maybe my first event could have been a little bit more chill, because we are not far from the store, and I can already see a small crowd of girls walking into the event. Bright lights shine from inside. My heart is starting to race as we walk through the door. A girl in a black dress wearing tall heels asks for our names. Jillian gives her our names. She thanks us and invites us to come in.

I glance around the store. Every girl looks like they came straight from getting blow-outs and their makeup done. They are all wearing little black dresses in differing styles. I look over at Jillian and notice that even she is wearing a black dress. I look down at my jeans and blazer, and I instantly feel out of place. I should have asked her what to wear.

There's a DJ in the corner playing music, champagne is being passed around along with silver trays full of appetizers. A TV camera crew setting up. Jillian whispers to me that NBC News is here and that probably means Kenneth Cole is here or on his way. My heart starts to beat faster. I don't know what he looks like, but I'm so excited to see him. Heels and boots are elegantly displayed all over the store. Girls are gushing over the new collection.

"Hello ladies, welcome. Do you two know about the newest 9.2.5. silver technology pumps and boots?" I turn around. Standing behind me is a stunning, immaculately groomed sales associate. She's rail-thin, wearing a tight-fitting black dress, and a pair of Kenneth Cole three-inch stilettos, making her seems taller than she really is. Her dark hair is pulled tight in a high ponytail that shows off her creamy pale complexion. She is pointing to one of the displays and waits for our response.

"No, we don't."

She gives us a wide smile. Her bright red lips make her teeth gleaming white. "Well, these shoes are very exclusive. No one has done this technology with heels before. The silver part at the bottom of the shoe helps keep the pressure off your foot so you can be comfortable in your heels all day long."

I have to admit that the heels are beautiful. They are a classic black leather pump with long, very skinny silver heels. I pick up one of the shoes and rub my fingers along the leather. It is so soft. I love them. They are very Hollywood glamorous.

"If you purchase any pair of heels or boots, we will give you a fifteen percent discount. But only during the event this evening."

I turn over the shoe to see the price. They are $150. Even with the discount, they are still way over $100, and I just can't buy another pair of expensive shoes. I have been putting too much on my credit card. I slowly put the heel back on display feeling a little bummed.

"Well, ladies. Let me know if I can get you a size." She gives us another smile and walks toward another group of girls.

As a server passes by, he stops to offer us champagne. We each take a glass, cheers, and take a sip. The store is getting really crowded. The music is getting louder as well.

"Ready to go mingle with me?"

"Sure."

"I'm just going to find some of the girls I know."

"Okay. I'll just follow you."

We head into the crowd of girls, and for the next twenty minutes, I'm being introduced to other Chicago bloggers, girls who are writers for *Michigan Avenue Magazine* and *CS Magazine*. A photographer comes by and asks to take our picture. He asks our names and tells us we may be in the next issue of *CS Magazine* and to look out for our photo. The music is suddenly turned down. A woman is at the microphone.

"Excuse me! Ladies and gentlemen. Excuse me! Can I have your attention? Hello. Excuse me. Just need your attention for a few minutes." The crowd begins to quiet down and turns to look at the lady at the microphone.

"Hello, everyone and thank you! Thank you for coming tonight and being a part of our newest collection here at Kenneth Cole. I want to introduce to you a very special guest this evening. He has taken the time from his busy schedule to come here to speak to you all about his newest shoe technology. I'm very excited to announce to you, Mr. Kenneth Cole!"

The crowd cheers and applauds as he makes his way to the microphone.

"Thank you, everyone! Thank you! Thank you so much for coming here to tonight. It's always so great to be in Chicago. It's such an amazing city."

I nod my head in agreement, and I feel chills. This is so cool! Kenneth Cole is actually here. This is one of the most exciting things that I have ever done. He speaks for the next few minutes about his newest shoe technology and how it will change the way that women wear heels.

Now, I really want a pair of these heels! I will have to save up. I need to be more responsible and stop charging everything to my credit card. When Kenneth Cole finishes speaking, he is whisked over to the reporters. The lady gets back on the microphone and tells us to stick around. There's still plenty of food and drinks. Kenneth will be around shortly to take photos.

I'm not a blogger, but I have to get a photo with him. It isn't every day that you have the chance to meet a famous fashion designer.

"Jillian, can we hang around for a bit? I really want to get a photo with Kenneth Cole."

"Sure, we can do that. Let's make our way over in a little bit after he is done with the press."

We make our rounds again, grab another champagne, and wait for Kenneth Cole. I see a crowd of girls heading in his direction.

"Jillian, let's go over. He just finished with the reporters."

"Okay. Let's go get that photo."

I grab Jillian's arm, we walk toward the crowd and stand in line for about ten minutes.

It's our turn to take a photo.

"Hello, ladies. Thank you for coming. What are your names?"

"I'm Kelly, and this is my friend Jillian."

"Nice to meet you both."

I'm grinning like a little kid as he holds out his arm to shake hands. I'm so not playing it cool at all.

"Would you ladies like to do a photo?"

"Umm, yes please."

"Kelly, I will take a photo of you, and then you can take one of me."

"Okay." I hand Jillian my iPhone.

We take the photos, thank him, and express how much we love the new collection. He gives us a *thank you*, and we walk away. I'm literally on cloud nine. What an awesome experience.

"Okay, we can go now if you want. I don't think the night can get much better than that."

"Okay, sounds good."

Michigan Avenue looks extra beautiful this evening. I don't want the evening to be over just yet. I want to stay here in this moment and enjoy being out in the city.

"Jillian, I can't thank you enough for inviting me. Tonight was so much fun."

"I'm so glad you had fun. That's basically how those events go. Although it's not every day you get to meet the designer. So, this was a great first one for you to go to."

"Well, I really loved every minute. It's still pretty early so do you want to grab another drink somewhere?"

"Sure. Let's go to this place in my neighborhood called *Le Colonial*. They have a lychee martini that is amazing and you will love."

"I've never had a lychee martini. I'm sure these are not like the cheap martini's at *SoPo*."

"No, they are not. If you like martini's, you will love these."

"Okay. Let's go there then." I stop for a moment. As quickly as I can, I switch out of my heels into a pair of flats I have in my purse.

"I learned this little tip from Kourtney, and it has changed my life."

"Ha! That is a really good tip."

I love the Gold Coast neighborhood. The white building of *Le Colonial* looks like someone's elegant mansion. The first floor has plenty of smaller white linen tables. It's a little busy as late diners are still enjoying their evening. We head upstairs to a quaint little bar. It is empty, so we take a seat on the stools at the bar.

"Hello, what can I get you, girls?"

"We are going to have two lychee martinis."

"Oh, excellent choice. They are the best."

"Yep. I've had a few here before, but my friend has never been here. I told her they are amazing."

"Well, welcome."

A few minutes later, she places two lychee martinis in front of us. "Cheers ladies. Enjoy!" The martinis are almost clear with a piece of lychee on the side of the glass.

"So, Jillian. What is lychee anyway?"

"It's a tropical sweet fruit."

"Oh."

I take a sip. My martini is sweet but not too sweet and very refreshing.

"Oh. This is so good!"

"Isn't it? It's one of my favorite drinks."

I could easily have a few of these lychee martinis. We take our time and enjoy our drink but decide one martini is enough for tonight. We thank our bartender, pay the tab, and head outside to catch a cab.

While in the cab on the way home, I am dazzled by this experience and grinning from ear to ear. I replay the night in my head. Somehow, I *must* have my own fashion blog. I love the combination of fashion and writing, so I just need to figure out how to make this happen. I wonder if Vin would be able to help me?

SIXTEEN

I couldn't be more excited! Spring is here and in full swing. Every day has been beautiful. Chicagoans are either in full baseball mode watching the Cubs or sitting out on café patios enjoying the sunshine and a cocktail or two. I, however, am in full blog-research mode. I have spent days looking at blog themes, studying my favorite blogs, and setting up Google alerts for all things Chicago. I casually tell Vin over lunch about my idea for my blog and ask how hard it would be to set up a WordPress blog. I'm hoping he can give me some direction.

"You just want a WordPress blog? That's not too complicated to do especially if the theme is simple enough. I could probably do it for you in a few hours. Have you picked out a theme you like?"

"Really? You would do that? Yeah, I'm choosing between two free themes I really like."

"What are you going to blog about?"

"Fashion and Chicago stuff. I just want to write about whatever I like."

"Just make sure you have a clear direction for your blog and be as niche as you can. Fashion is very broad."

"I think I'm just going to write a few posts and see what direction I want to go."

"Well, decide on a theme, the colors, and a name. If you are free to meet on Saturday, I can help you set up everything."

"Really? You would do all that for me?"

"Yep, it's no problem."

"Wow, thank you so much. I really appreciate all your help."

I had no idea he would offer to help me. I thought he would guide me in the right direction or suggest someone who would be able to help me. This is seriously so nice of him especially since he is busy running the agency.

Our original intent for lunch was to discuss the team achieving its goal. We are due for another company outing. Since it's baseball season, and pretty much everyone in the office is a die-hard Cubs fan. James and Vin decide it would be fun to take the team to a baseball game but not at the stadium. It worked out best to buy tickets for one of the rooftops, which also included unlimited food and drinks.

"So, anyway, I looked up a few Cub games. Next Friday, there is a game at 1:05. I think the team will love to go. It's such a fun idea for a team outing."

"You are going to get everyone rooftop tickets?"

"Yeah."

"Okay. When we get back from lunch, go ahead and get those tickets."

"Okay, will do."

I book tickets for the entire office as soon as I get back to the office. I send James and Vin an instant message to tell them everything is taken care of.

Before I left work, James asked me if I wanted to meet him at *SoPo* tonight, but I can't. I'm spending this evening finalizing my blog theme and the colors, and I need to decide on a name. I have written down a few names that I like. I want something personal and something that is related to fashion. In my notebook of scribbled names, one name keeps coming back to me that is quirky and fun: My Posh Jeans. Victoria Beckham is hands-down my favorite celebrity and style icon. I loved the Spice Girls when I was growing up. *Posh* was Victoria Beckham's nickname, and it's still pretty much her nickname today. I had purchased a pair of her jeans, and I had the chance to meet her at Saks that same day. It was a major highlight of my life and a very memorable experience. I feel my style is casual and chic like hers and somehow the name just fits.

As I sat on the couch eating pizza, the rest of my vision for my blog just came to life. I've chosen a name for my blog, and now I need a theme. I look over the two that I like. The one I keep going back to is simple, mostly white, and positions the logo at the top. It seems the best look for My Posh Jeans. Check that off my list. I take a few more bites of my pizza.

I look over my list. I'm down to two colors, blue and purple. I love blue, but purple seems right for fashion. I don't want my blog too pinkish-purple, so I Google "purple color" in the image search. I take some more bites of my pizza as I look through different shades of purple. I stop at one I like. I look at the name. Royal purple. Of course, it's perfect. I recheck my notes. Wow, I did it! I sit back on the couch feeling super excited. I have completed everything on my list, and now I can't wait for tomorrow morning.

"So, David, I'm going to a coffee shop called *Intelligentsia Coffee* on Broadway. Vin is going to help me set up my blog."

My brother is standing there in the living room smiling at me with his arms crossed. "Okay, have fun."

I roll my eyes at him. I don't care what he thinks. I'm so appreciative that Vin is going to help me get my blog up and running. It's generous of him to take the time, especially on a Saturday.

I walk over to *Intelligentsia*. I have a bounce in my step. It's a beautiful May day. I'm so excited to work on my blog. I head down Broadway, and I am loving the walk. Broadway is lined with fun restaurants, bars, and little shops. This is my first time going to *Intelligentsia*. It's a modern-style coffee shop with plenty of tables. I choose a table in the front and take a seat. I look around to see if Vin is already here. He's not yet. I go over all my notes, and he strolls in about ten minutes later.

He greets me with a little hug. "Hey, sorry I'm late. I was looking for parking. It seems like everyone is out today."

"That's okay. I just got here."

"Wait. Is that your laptop? Oh, Kelly." I look down at my clunky, outdated giant of a laptop that I've had since college.

"If you are going to have a great blog, you are going to need a better laptop, especially if you are going to be writing out of your apartment. You don't want to be carrying that thing around all the time."

"I know. I will get a new one sometime. I don't have much cash for one right now." I sigh to myself. Another thing to add to the credit card. "Okay, well let me get you a coffee. It's the least I can do for you helping me today. What do you like?"

"Thanks. I'll have a cappuccino."

"Okay. I'll be right back."

I order a vanilla latte for myself and a cappuccino for Vin. I bring our coffees to our table. I sit back in my seat and take a sip of coffee. It's sweet from the vanilla, but the coffee is smooth and delicious.

"Like it?"

"Hmm, I do. It's really good."

"Good. It's my favorite coffee in the city."

We install my theme, edit the blog, and change all the colors to make everything exactly my style. A few hours later, *My Posh Jeans* is up and running! It's just how I imagined. My blog couldn't be more perfect.

"What do you think?"

"It's so great! I'm excited. I can't wait to get home and set up everything else."

"Good. That part should be pretty easy for you."

"Thank you so much. I really owe you."

"It's no problem. Honestly. I've been doing this stuff for years."

"So, are you hungry? As I was walking here, I saw this cute little brunch place across the street. Do you want to go check it out? It's my treat for you helping me today."

"Okay, yeah, I'm pretty hungry."

We pack up our things and walk across the street to *Mortar and Pestle*. The host shows us to a little two-top table along the wall. I love rustic décor and lots of lacquered wood. Tiny flowers in little vases are on every table.

"What do you think you are going to get? The biscuits with jam look really good."

"Yeah, I saw those too, and maybe some eggs?"

"Same. Let's order that."

We give the server our order, and she brings us some fresh coffee.

"So, what are your plans for the rest of the day. I know I'm going home to work on my blog."

"Hmm, not sure. I might be meeting up with some friends."

Our food arrives. We agree that the biscuits are a smart choice. We finish off our quick brunch, and Vin offers to drop me off at my apartment, so I don't have to carry my giant laptop all the way home.

I spend the next few hours setting up my social media, navigating my blog, and creating an "About Me" page and "Contact" page. Now it's time to write my first post. I stare at my screen. My mind is blank. What should my first post be about? I'm thinking. How do I start it? I look at my phone. I've been sitting here for twenty minutes. This is a lot harder than I thought. I look through some of my favorite blogs that I follow to get some inspiration. Their posts look so professional. They have beautiful images. They write about their outfits and the latest styles for spring. I do love fashion, but these bloggers seem to know so much more than me.

Okay, don't get down, I say to myself. You have come this far. You can totally do this. I'm sure other bloggers didn't start out with gorgeous posts. I just need to write about me, who I am, and just be honest. Oh, wait! I got it! My first post should be about how I came up with the name for my blog, how I met Victoria Beckham and bought a pair of her jeans. That was a fun day, an interesting story, and it's a perfect introduction post. I spent the next few hours writing my post and deciding out how to make it look just perfect.

It's early evening when I'm ready to hit publish. This is it. My first blog post. I'm excited and so proud of myself. Will anyone read it? I call Mum to ask her to read it, and I send her the link. I'm too excited not to tell someone.

I share my first post on my Twitter account. I start following as many Chicagoans as I can find. I spend the rest of the night watching *Sweet Home Alabama* on the E! channel as I work on my social media and think up blog topics. It feels official. I could be a Chicago blogger.

SEVENTEEN

I work on my blog every chance I get. I also spend a lot of time on social media. I love following my favorite bloggers and celebrities to see what they are up to. Some fellow Chicagoans and Chicago places are starting to follow me back. When I'm not writing, I'm reading everything I can about blogging and building up my social media following.

Before I know it, it's Friday. Cubs game day. We are leaving early from work so we can head up to Wrigleyville. The whole office is excited about the game. I've only been to one Cubs game in my life, and I have never been to a game on one of the rooftops. It sounds like a lot of fun. I also have an idea for a blog post. I'm going to write about how to dress for a Cubs game.

We all leave the office around eleven and take the Red Line up to the Addison, which is also the "L" station stop for *Wrigley Field*. It's a beautiful spring day, perfect weather for a baseball game. On the train, everyone is in a great mood. As we continue north, the Red Line is filling up with excited Cubs fans in their Cubs caps, shirts, jerseys or hoodies. The conversation is all about the Cubs and what they need to do this season to win the World Series. While we are on the train, I tell Jillian all about my blog.

"Oh, that's really cool! I had no idea you wanted to start one. You will have to show me."

"I will. I know, I wanted to tell you, but I wanted to have it up and running first before I said anything."

"I will definitely start following you on social media."

"Thanks! I also might need you take a few photos of me today if you don't mind. I want to write a post about dressing for a Cubs game."

"Oh. That's a cute idea! I don't mind."

The train doors open at Addison. The crowd scrambles off and down the stairs. It's a mad rush to the bars for a few drinks before the game starts. Our group reaches the stadium and walks down Sheffield Avenue to what looks like a normal three-flat. We head inside, up the stairs, and into a giant room. It's set up with tables and chairs and a large buffet full of all kinds of stadium food. They have hot dogs and hamburgers with every fixing you could imagine. There's an ice cream machine with a setup of different toppings. I walk up another set of stairs to the rooftop. They're about ten rows of stadium chairs. A few of the guys are already figuring out the best place to sit to watch the game.

I look out to the baseball field. It's definitely a cool view. The stadium is filling up, and they're a few players warming up on the field. *Wrigley Field* has tons of energy, and although they have done a few updates to the stadium, it still has that old ballpark vibe including the famous ivy that is now filled in along the walls. I take a few photos on my iPhone and head back inside to grab some food. I fill my plate with a Chicago style hotdog and a handful of potato chips, then follow James, Vin, and Jillian back up to the rooftop.

Today couldn't be more perfect! I am with my friends and co-workers, eating a hotdog and chips, the sunshine is warm on my face, and I can hear all the sounds of a baseball game. The crack of the bat hitting a ball, the cheers in the crowd when the Cubs score, the echo of the game announcer, and the organ music that plays between innings. The Cubs are leading the game, and I can feel the energy emanating from the stadium. The whole afternoon is a blast, and I watched more of the game then I thought I would.

It's a great end to our company outing because the Cubs win! The crowd roars when the last run is scored, and that is when we slowly start to make our way out. James tells us he is meeting up with some friends at a place called *Parson's* in the Logan Square neighborhood. I've never heard of *Parson's* and I haven't been over to Logan Square yet. James tells me they have a huge backyard-style patio, amazing cocktails, and famous fried chicken. Since it's still really nice out and it's a new place for me to try, I tell him I will tag along.

"I'm in too. I'll just cab back to the Gold Coast later."

"Okay great. Vin?" Vin is looking down at his phone. James tries again.

"Hello, Vin! What are you going to do?"

"Oh, probably just head home and see what my friends are up to tonight."

"Okay. But did you hear us? Just so you know, you're welcome to come with us to *Parson's* if you want to go in that direction. My friends have an area on the patio, and we can join them."

"Okay, yeah, I'll come."

Since Wrigleyville is crazy right now, and to make the most of the weather, we decide to walk away from the stadium and bars before we catch a cab over to Logan Square. We walk among the crowds as fans are heading to the bars around the stadium. Finally, after a few months of living in Chicago, I've come to enjoy walking around the city. With the right pair of shoes, of course.

Vin, Jillian, and I are on the patio and pick up the menus to look over the food and cocktails.

"What are you guys going to get?"

"Probably just stick with beer or have a whiskey on the rocks."

"You don't want one of their frozen cocktails? It's the perfect day for one. What about you Jillian?"

"Yeah I'm getting one. I'm getting the Negroni Slushy."

"I will too. Anything refreshing always looks good."

The waitress comes by and takes our order.

"James, this place is really cool. I love the patio. It's so fun. I'm so glad you guys got this great spot. Thanks for letting us join you."

"Yeah, of course."

I sip my frozen cocktail and take in everything that is around me. I feel a light breeze and the late afternoon sun on my body. I listen to the all the sounds: the chatter of the people around me, the music playing on the speakers, and the cheering from a game of ping pong happening, in one corner of the patio. The restaurant is filling up. It's a happy start to the weekend.

"So, Kell. Have you seen any new movies lately?" Vin is almost looking down as he talks to me. He does not want to draw attention to our conversation.

"No. I've actually been working really hard on my blog. I'm having so much fun, and I've been spending all my free time on it."

"Cool. I have to take a look. But, if you're free maybe tomorrow and want to take a break, maybe we could go see another movie?"

I pause for a few seconds. I did want to go to a movie. I did have a lot of fun last time. But I didn't want it to get around the office that I'm hanging out with Vin by myself . . . alone. I quickly look around at our group. No one is paying attention.

"Okay, sure. I would love to." He gives me a smile, and I smile back.

It's Saturday, and I've been working for hours on my blog, and I'm starving. It's almost four, and I have hardly had a thing to eat all day. I hear a ping on my phone and see that I have a text from Vin.

What are you up to? Are you done working yet? Take a break.

Yes! I'm ready to take a break. I'm starving. I'm craving Mexican food. Do you want to go to Cesar's on Broadway? I saw it the other day, and I want to try their food.

Yep. I know the place. I'll be over in twenty.

Vin comes to get me, and I'm really excited to be going to dinner with him. I'm not sure if that's a good thing. It's a quick drive to *Cesar's* from my apartment, and we are lucky to find a parking spot close to the restaurant. It is not too busy yet, but it is also early in the evening.

"I've heard that the margaritas here are good, but they're also really strong. I wonder if they are as good as *Mercadito? Mercadito* is definitely my favorite so far."

"Let's have one and find out."

The server greets us with a bowl of chips and salsa, and we order two frozen margaritas with salt. I dive into the chips.

"Wow, you must be hungry."

"I haven't really eaten anything all day."

"Yeah, it looks like it. So, how's the blog going?"

"It's good. I've been working on it a lot. I just wrote a post today about how to dress for a Cubs game."

"Oh, that's a good idea."

"Yeah. It turned out well. I gave some advice on what to wear if you don't have Cubs gears or if you're visiting Chicago and you want to go to a Cubs game."

"Wow, you are now a true Chicago blogger."

"Ha, ha! I hope so. One day."

Our margaritas arrive, and they look refreshing. We both take a sip. They are good, but not as good as *Mercadito*, but it is definitely a yummy margarita.

"I know I can't have too many of these. They are really strong." Our server comes back, and we order some food.

"So, I haven't had the chance yet to tell you about my date."

The words instantly make my heart stop. "Oh. Wait. What? No, you haven't. When was this?"

"It was last weekend. On Saturday." Saturday? His date must have been after he helped me with my blog.

"A friend set us up. She has hung out with us a few times at Leg Room. I didn't really want to go, but I decided last minute to just go and have drinks."

"Oh, how was it? Did you have fun?"

"Yeah. It was okay. She was nice. But I don't think it will go anywhere. Not really interested. We went for a walk after, and she tried to kiss me. I wasn't really into it, so that's how the date ended."

"Oh."

That's all I can think of to say. I have no idea why I'm being so weird. I honestly have no interest in dating Vin. But I feel relieved that his date didn't go so well. I think it's because I'm just a tiny bit jealous that if he starts dating again, we won't hang out as much.

Of course, it would probably be the same for me if I met someone.

"You're not saying anything."

"Oh, sorry. It's just, umm, sorry it didn't go well. I'm sure you will find someone soon."

"I'm not too worried about dating right now. I just wanted to tell you because I think we have become pretty good friends."

"Of course. We are. I'm sorry, really. You can tell me anything. I'm glad you told me."

"Good. So what movie should we see after this?"

We both want to watch an older movie on TV instead of going to the theater. We talked before about our love for '80s movies, and we think it will be fun to watch one that neither of us has seen. Netflix has a lot of old movies, so we agree to go to my apartment since we are so close, and my brother is back in the suburbs again. We search through Netflix and find, *The Burbs* starring Tom Hanks.

"Oh my gosh, I absolutely love Tom Hanks. He is truly one of my favorite actors. I can't believe neither of us has seen this movie. I'll make some popcorn, and then we can watch."

I watch Vin as he gets the movie ready and gets comfortable on the couch. I bring the popcorn over, grab my blanket, and get settled on the couch next to him.

"Ready?"

"I'm ready." I wrap myself in my blanket and Vin starts the movie.

We both enjoyed *The Burbs*. It's funny and a typical '80s movie. The credits are rolling, and Vin suddenly jumps up and starts putting on his shoes.

"Sorry, Kell. I have to go."

"Really. Why?"

"I'll see you on Monday. Okay? Good pick, right? We can watch another one soon." Vin is suddenly acting strangely. He heads over to my front door and opens it. I look up at him confused as he is standing in my doorway.

"Okay. Yeah."

"Bye." He closes my front door and just like that he is gone.

I sit and stare at my front door for a few seconds wondering what had just happened. Maybe he is just joking and will be right back? I sit there waiting for another minute. Nothing.

Okay, stop being so weird. It's not like he just walked out on a date with me. This wasn't a date, and it's not like he ditched me. We had plans to see a movie, and we did. Maybe he forgot he is late for something and he has other plans? That totally makes sense but why wouldn't he just say that? Why leave so abruptly? I think about texting him but what would I say? I look at the time, it's almost ten, and I decided to just head to bed.

My brother comes home late on Sunday. I tell him about the Cubs rooftop game on Friday and how much fun it was. I also tell him about last night. He gave me a strange look.

"Well, if you want to know what I think. I think your boss likes you. He sure wants to hang out with you a lot."

"No, he absolutely doesn't. We are just friends and, anyway, I'm not going to date my boss. Plus, I don't like him in that way. And, if he did like me so much, why would he just leave like that? That doesn't make any sense."

"I don't know. Maybe he didn't want to feel like he was pushing you or didn't want anything to go too far. He knows he's the boss."

"No. I don't think so. He doesn't even sit close to me or anything like that. Besides, him leaving like that just proves that he doesn't like me. I just thought it was weird, so that's why I brought it up to you. I'm not upset or anything. Anyway. How was your weekend at home?"

"Well, it was *good*. But, I have something to tell you."

EIGHTEEN

You know the feeling when everything in your life is going extremely well. You are really happy, and everything seems to be going your way. A part of you starts to wonder if things will stay this way or if something will come along and completely mess things up for you.

Well, lately, I'm feeling exactly this way. Everything has been going well with work and with my new friends. I'm starting to become more comfortable in my surroundings, and I feel more confident walking around and exploring the city. I'm having fun, and I'm enjoying my new life in the city.

As soon as my brother says the words, I know exactly what's coming.

"What's up? What do you have to tell me." I look up at him as I slowly sit down on the couch.

"Well, I've been thinking about this for a while, and I'm just not happy here in the city. I don't know anyone. My job doesn't pay well, and it's hard for me to pay for things. I'm tired of being stressed out and unhappy all the time. I talked to Mum and Dad this weekend, and I think it's best for me if I move home."

Yep, everything did seem a little too good to be true, and just like that everything is now about to be completely turned upside down for me. When I hear the news, to be honest, I'm not at all that surprised. However, suddenly everything feels unfair, and I'm in a little bit of a panic.

I don't say anything, but I continue to look at my brother as he's talking. I do feel bad for him. I can tell that lately he hasn't been happy. After all, he had moved here to help me. He had wanted to try something new, but he's also doing me a huge favor by being my roommate. I don't want him to feel this bad because of my dream, but this news is really going to affect me in every way. I can't afford to pay for the rent by myself. I may be a little dramatic, but I don't want to move back home and commute to the office every day. I love the life I'm making for myself in the city. There is no way I want to move back to the suburbs. My life is here. I'm quiet for a few minutes so I can think of what to say. I don't want this to start a fight with him.

"Okay. So, when do you think you will move back?"

"I think next weekend."

"What! Next weekend? Are you serious? That doesn't give me much time to figure out things. What am I going to do for rent next month? It's due in a few days."

"I will pay for June. Then, by July, maybe you can move or get a roommate?"

I shake my head. "I know you're unhappy here, but I just feel like this is going to really mess things up for me. Especially financially."

I take a deep breath and continue. "I'm sorry the city is not where you want to be. It makes me sad to think that you are so unhappy. Of course, I want you to be happy. But. Ugh! This just really, really sucks. So, when you told Mum and Dad, what did they say?"

"They said they just want me to be happy. They want both of us to be happy. They know you love it here. But, they also know that I come home almost every weekend and that the city life is just not meant for me."

Tears start forming in my eyes. I put my head in my hands to cover my face.

"Don't cry. I'm sorry. I just feel so stressed out, and I don't want to live like this."

"Yeah. I get it. I don't want you to be this stressed or unhappy. Okay, let's talk in a day or so. I just need to figure some things out. I need to think about what I'm going to do."

I get up and start walking toward my bedroom. "At least now maybe I can have a room with closet."

"Kelly don't be mad."

"I'm not mad. I just need time to think about all of this." I walk into my room and close the door.

I walk into the office the next day, and I feel like a zombie. I sit down at my desk and let out a huge sigh. Maybe I'm overreacting, but I feel so overwhelmed, and I can't think of what to do.

All morning I found myself staring into space. I try to focus on what I have to do, but I can't concentrate on work, not today. I'm not my usual bubbly self, and my friends start to notice by lunchtime.

"Hey, you want to go to our sushi spot today?"

"Maybe."

"What's going on with you? What's wrong. You've been quiet today. You didn't even come by and say hi this morning."

"I know. I'm sorry. It's just that my brother came home last night and told me he is moving out. Next weekend. I just don't know what to do. I can't afford to pay all the rent. My credit card bill is already high. After moving here, I wiped out all my savings, so I just don't know what to do."

"Whoa, that's a tough situation. I mean the easiest thing to do is to get a roommate. It would only be for like six months unless you want to stay in that place. Or you could sublease or try to get out of your lease and get a studio. I live in a studio, and I love it."

I haven't even thought about a studio. Jillian lives in a great neighborhood, and I would love to live downtown.

"If you don't mind me asking, how much is your rent?"

"Fifteen hundred."

"We pay twelve hundred for our place, so I definitely can't pay that."

"Yeah, I understand. I live in a good location in the Gold Coast. So that's why."

"Thanks for your advice though. I definitely do have a few options, so I guess I need to figure out what works best for me."

"Yep, no problem. So, do you want to get some food?"

"No. Thanks though. I'm not really that hungry."

"Okay, then. See you in a bit."

I take a break from my desk and walk to the kitchen to warm up the coffee I barely touched. Amy stops me as I walk by.

"Hey Kelly, we overheard you telling Jillian something about your brother leaving. What are you going to do?"

"I have no idea, Amy. I have a few options, I guess. But I just don't know."

"I hope you figure it all out. Let's all go out this weekend for some drinks and help you get your mind off things."

"Thanks. I'd really love that."

I give Amy a weak smile and head into the kitchen. Vin is at the microwave heating up some food.

"Hey, will you come into my office when you are done?"

"Okay." I keep my head down to avoid making eye contact with him.

I heat up my coffee and slowly walk toward Vin's office. "Shut the door."

I give him a worried look, turn around, and shut the door behind me.

"Did I do something wrong?"

"No. I just wanted to talk to you about the other night. I didn't mean to just get up and leave like that."

"Oh yeah. Hmm, it's okay. I had forgotten for a second all about what happened on Saturday night. Saturday night now seems like ages ago.

"No, I want to explain. I just felt a little off. Maybe it was from the food, so I just had to get home. I was embarrassed. I should have said something. I'm sure it looked strange, so I'm sorry."

"Oh. Oh, I see. I hope you feel better now. That's an awful feeling."

"All good now. I just didn't know what to say and how to leave. I should have texted you, but I just thought it would come out weird. Anyway. I just wanted you to know. I didn't want you to think I would normally just leave like that. So, anyway, what's up with you today? Something wrong? Are you upset with me?"

"No. No. Nothing with you. My brother came home last night and told me he was moving home."

"Oh. Really?"

"Yeah, and the thing is, he said he is moving home this weekend. He will give me the rent for June and then I'm on my own. I can't afford the apartment by myself, and so I'm a little overwhelmed as to what to do."

"I can see that."

"I love my life here in the city. I love my job here. I've just started to make friends, started my blog, and things are going really well. I absolutely don't want to have to move home and commute here."

"No, you don't want to do that."

"No, I really don't."

"Hmm, that's tough. Let me know how I can help you. Honestly, I'd try to get out of your lease if you don't want a roommate. I would tell him about the two-bedroom thing. Your room is not a bedroom. It might be hard to get a roommate with that room."

"Maybe. That might actually be a good idea. Jillian said I could get my own place, a studio or something. But, she pays way more than I do now, so I don't know how that will work."

"Oh, I have no doubt we could find something that could work for you."

"We?"

"Yeah, I can definitely help you, whatever you need."

"Thanks. I really appreciate it. I don't have much time to decide, but I do want to think for a few days about what to do. My gut is telling me that I don't want to find a roommate. It could take too long, and it would only be for six months. Plus, with the bedroom with no closet, who would want that? I'm not sure I want to continue living in that room either. With my brother moving out, I would rather have his room. I'm not sure I want to live with someone I don't know. I would love to live downtown. That would be an absolute dream. That's actually been my dream since I was little."

"Well, I can go with you to look at places if you want."

"Okay, thanks. I'll let you know. I should head back to my desk."

David and I don't talk much the rest of the week. I don't want it to be that way, but I feel like I'm being let down. It's the start of Memorial Day weekend, and we have off work on Monday. While it feels like the rest of the city is celebrating the beginning of summer, I'm helping my brother and his friends move his things out of the apartment.

At least tonight I'm going out with the girls to *RPM Italian.* After the week I've had and helping my brother move out, I'm ready for a night out to enjoy a few cocktails. Amy's boyfriend's brother is in town, and she really wants me to meet him. I am not really in the mood to meet a guy, but I agree to go because I like Amy a lot and have a lot of fun with her. I'm determined to enjoy a night out and not think about my current situation.

"Okay, David. You got everything?"

"Yeah, I think so. Thank you for helping."

"Sure. I will see you next time I come home. Tell Mum and Dad I said hi."

"Okay. I'm so sorry that everything worked out this way."

"It's okay. I will figure it out. Thank you for the money for June."

We give each other a tight hug, and he heads out with his friends. He is my brother after all. I can't be mad at him forever. It did make me sad to see how upset he has been. I can't imagine living somewhere that makes you miserable.

After they are gone, I sit in the quiet apartment. I don't have the energy to move my things into his bedroom, and I am still not sure what I'm going to do. The roommate thing is not at the top of my list. So, either I get out of my lease or I sublet. I think that I will try to get out of my lease.

We are all meeting at *RPM Italian* around seven. I'm super excited to go to *RPM*, because I'm a huge fan of Giuliana and Bill Rancic. They co-own the restaurant and maybe they would be there? On social media, I've often seen that they ate there.

I take my time getting ready and get in a cab about fifteen minutes before seven. I arrive at the restaurant right after seven. I tell the host I'm meeting some friends. She tells me to feel free to look around. We have plans to have some drinks and appetizers at the bar.

As I walk around the bar at *RPM Italian*, I notice it's very modern and chic. I spot my group sitting at the corner of the bar.

"Hey, Kelly! I don't think you have met my boyfriend, Brett, and this is his brother Brian."

"Hi! Nice to meet you guys."

Amy moves over so I can sit next to Brian. Everyone looks over at me and smiles.

"So, how's it going? Did your brother move out today?"

"Yeah, he did. I'm going to call my landlord on Tuesday and see what my options are."

"That sounds like a good place to start. I really hope you can figure things out."

"Me too. But tonight, I don't want to think about all that. I need a drink." I look at the menu and order a glass of prosecco. It's Giuliana's prosecco so, of course, I want to try it.

I'm having such a good time hanging out with everyone. I'm feeling more relaxed now, and it's so nice to be out. Amy asks everyone if we're ready for another round of drinks and if we want to order some food. I look up to find the bartender, and I instantly see that familiar face.

Vin is standing across the room at the other side of the bar with Vince whom I met at Leg Room. They are ordering drinks. I watch as they pick up their drinks from the bar and head in our direction.

"Hey, guys. Why is Vin here?"

Natalie looks over at me and waves him over. "Oh, I invited him.

I text him earlier to see what he was doing, and he said he didn't really have plans, so I told him we would all be here."

I instantly feel so awkward. I'm not doing anything wrong, just having drinks with friends. But, I feel like Vin is going to be so different with me because I'm sitting here with another guy.

Vin and Vince approach our corner at the bar, and Natalie gets up right away and gives Vin a hug. "Hi! I'm so glad you came!"

Vin gives her a slight hug back and says hello to the rest of us. He locks eyes with me, gives me a brief smile, and looks away. I know he feels awkward. He totally thinks I'm on a date. It looks like I'm on a date.

Natalie is at the end of our group, so Vin and Vince stand next to her. I try to make eye contact with Vin again, but it's hard to look down the bar toward him, and Natalie is giving him all her attention. She is flipping her hair and leaning into him. I take a sip of my prosecco and look up at the ceiling.

I don't want to date Vin. But I didn't want him to date Natalie either. I also don't want him to think I'm interested in in this guy, Brian. I know I'm selfish not wanting anything to change between us. All I wanted to do is have fun tonight, and now I just feel annoyed. I try a few more times to get Vin's attention, but it's impossible with Natalie next to him.

Our appetizers arrive, and we get another round of drinks. We ordered the Brussels sprouts, the Giuliana's Italian salad, focaccia, and the meatballs. The meatballs are famous, and they are really delicious.

We finish our drinks and food, and the group decides to go somewhere else. We have been taking up the bar for a while. I get up to use the restroom. I'm not sure I want to go somewhere else and watch Natalie and Vin together. I head back out of the bathroom and Vin is standing outside.

"Hey."

"Hey."

"Are you going to come out with us. I think we are going to head to Leg Room."

"Umm, I'm not sure. It's been a long day, and so I think I'm ready to head out."

"Oh. Okay. How's your date going?"

"My date? No. He's not my date. That's Amy's boyfriend's brother. He's just in town for the weekend."

"Oh."

"Well, you seem to be having a lot of fun with Natalie." Oh geez, that sounded really bratty.

"She's okay. I told you before, she's fun and nice."

"Yeah, she is." We stand in silence for a few seconds.

"Oh. So, I think I'm going to take your advice and call my landlord. She what my options are. If I can get out of my lease, maybe you can go with me to see a few places?"

"Sure, I said I would go with you."

"Okay, well, have fun at Legroom." I leave him standing there and head back to the bar.

"You guys. I think I'm going to head out. It's been a long day for me." I pay my portion of the bill and give each one of the girls a hug.

"Are you sure you want to leave?"

"Yeah, I'm sure. I'm just feeling tired. Thank you so much for including me. It's been a fun night. Brian, it was so nice to meet and chat with you. Hope to see you again next time you are in town."

"You too, Kelly." I grab my purse and my leather jacket and head out of the restaurant.

I'm sitting at home on Tuesday evening, and I'm very nervous. I go over and over in my head what to say. I know I have to make this call. Once I know what my options are, I can decide what to do. I take a deep breath and call my landlord. A man finally answers after about seven rings and mumbles "hello".

"Hi. This is Kelly from the 2F apartment on George Street." I wait for a response. The man mumbles "yep". So, I continue.

"I'm really sorry to bother you, but I was wondering if I could talk to you for a few moments about my lease. I can no longer afford the rent by myself, and I'm finding it very difficult to find a room-mate because the second bedroom doesn't have a closet. I have read that in order to rent the second bedroom as bedroom, it must have a closet."

My landlord makes a groaning sound. "If you want to break your lease, I will just keep your deposit. Does that sound okay?"

"Yes! Umm. Yes, that would be fine. Thank you."

The second bedroom not really being a second bedroom has worked! Not getting my deposit back is better than having to fully break my lease.

"If you don't mind, could I please get that in writing?"

He mumbles that the receptionist would email me in the morning and tells me I have to be out by June 30th.

"No problem and thank you."

Oh my gosh! I did it! I got out of my lease. I wasn't going to get my deposit back to put on another apartment, but I would figure that out. I feel so relieved! Now, it's time to start looking for a new home. This also meant I could stay in the city! I send a text to Vin.

I did it! I got out of my lease! The 2nd bedroom thing worked! Thank you so much for the advice!

No problem. Let's find you an apartment.

NINETEEN

I had forgotten how frustrating it is to search for an apartment, especially again with a limited budget. This time, I'm really not wanting to pay more than a thousand per month for my rent. This is the very most I can afford on my own. I have gone to see a few places with and without Vin after work.

So far, I have seen a place on LaSalle Street that is under my budget, but the studio was really, really tiny, and it wasn't updated at all. I had gone with Vin to the Belden Stratford to look at their apartments. The building used to be a hotel, and I love it and all the amazing historical décor, however, the studio that was available was very dark and still felt very much like a hotel room. I also went to see a new apartment building that is gorgeous and, of course, it's totally out of my price range. But I wanted to see what I could get if I could eventually afford more than a thousand per month.

I'm driving with Vin, and we are heading to a few appointments. I'm getting a little nervous that I won't find a place. I only have two weeks left in my apartment. That morning, I found a few more places on craigslist that look promising, and I asked him if he wouldn't mind taking me since it would be faster for him to drive me than to take public transport all over the city.

My first appointment is to look at two units in the same building on Clark Street in Lincoln Park at ten forty-five and eleven-fifteen, and the other apartment is downtown at noon on Delaware Place. I looked up the building on Delaware Place and saw that it's behind the *John Hancock Building* and really close to Michigan Avenue. Being a block from Michigan Avenue is an absolute dream of mine. The downside is it's another boutique hotel converted into all studios. Hopefully, these units won't still look like hotel rooms.

The two units on Clark Street are really nice. They are in a good location and within my budget. The manager of the building tells me I should act quickly. June is a popular month, and these two could be rented by the end of the day. I tell him I just have to see one more place, and I will get back to him as soon as possible. Since I would love to be downtown, something's telling me, I must see the one downtown on Delaware before I make my decision.

I'm feeling positive. Vin and I head downtown, park over by the Gold Coast and walk over to Michigan Avenue and Delaware Place. Delaware is a very quiet street especially for being so close to Michigan Avenue. As we walk toward the address, I start to feel really excited. I absolutely love all these vintage buildings. Each building has its own character with beautiful flowers and bushes perfectly manicured along the front.

We walk into the building. A young man is sitting at the front desk. The lobby looks just like a vintage boutique hotel. They have maintained all the character of the hotel, and you can tell it has been updated with fresh decor, paint, and wallpaper.

"Hello. I'm here to see one of your studios."

"Oh yes. Your name please?"

"Kelly."

"Okay, Kelly. Please wait one moment, and I will be right back."

He returns a few minutes later with a clipboard, walks around the lobby desk, and pushes the button to the elevator.

"Okay, come up with me." A small elevator door opens, and he pushes the button for ten. We slowly head up to the floor.

"This building was built in 1927 and used to be a hotel, and now every unit is an updated apartment. The building right next door is a boutique hotel. They have a very popular rooftop bar called *Drumbar* and an excellent restaurant which is very convenient. This building is a sixteen story, studio-only building. The building has a rooftop deck and a fitness center on the top floor. Full laundry is on the basement floor." We reach the tenth floor, and the door slowly opens.

"I apologize for the elevator. It's original with the building, and it's consider to be a lift." We walk out into the hallway, and he uses a key card to open the door right across from the elevator.

"This is one of our biggest studios. Each resident gets two key cards for their apartment, and it also works on the front entrance door. Since this used to be a hotel, the developer just thought we could still use the key card system instead of replacing all the locks."

"That's really cool."

The young guy opens the door, and the three of us walk in. "Now, this unit has just been freshly painted and cleaned and is ready to rent now."

I look around the studio. I can smell the fresh paint, and everything looks brand new. To the left of a door is a tiny little kitchenette. It's brand new and updated, and it even has a dishwasher. Something I don't have now. The living and bedroom area is a large square, and it's a nice size. The windows face Delaware, which I like, and there's lots of natural light. I walk through a doorway, and there's a large walk-in open closet. To the left is a door to the bathroom. I walk back out grinning from ear to ear. This place is absolutely perfect.

"How much is the rent?"

"Well, all our units include cable, internet, and all utilities except for electric. The total per month for this unit is $1030."

"Wow, all of that is included?"

"Yep, except for electric." I look at Vin, and he nods back.

"Okay, where do I sign?"

We leave my new apartment building, and I don't think I can be happier. Everything is working out okay. I'm now going to be in an even better apartment than before, and it's in my dream location. The management of most apartment buildings are now asking for a move-in-fee instead of a deposit. That works out so much better for me since I'm losing my deposit on my other apartment. I just had to pay my move-in-fee today and in a few days my rent for July.

"We should celebrate. Let's go somewhere for a drink in your new neighborhood."

"Really? You want to?"

"Yeah, of course, let's do it. Anywhere you have been wanting to go."

"Well, there's somewhere I've really been wanting to go. Are you sure anywhere?"

"Yep. Let's go."

A few minutes later we walk into *The Drake Hotel*. I've been dying to look inside this hotel as it's a famous landmark hotel. My mum told me it's where Princess Diana stayed when she visited Chicago. I remember watching it all on TV. The lobby is just as I imagined. It's gorgeous. I'm not sure where we can get a drink. So, we head up the stairs to the restaurant and ask one of the servers. He tells us we can either have a drink here in the Palm Court or at the bar downstairs. That sounds fun. We thank him and take the stairs all the way back to the ground level.

Around the corner, we walk down the ground level hallway, and into a bar called *Coq d'Or*. The bar is dark and very old. The bartender tells us to take a seat wherever we like, and he will be right with us. There is only another couple in the bar. It's early in the afternoon, so I'm not surprised. The bartender comes over a few minutes later with some waters, and we ask him about the bar. He tells us it's a speakeasy and one of the oldest bars in the city. Vin orders a whiskey, and I order a lemon drop martini. It was a little early in the day, but that's okay, I like my martini's, and it's time to celebrate.

The next Saturday, James and Vin and I move my bed, a few pieces of furniture, my clothes, and a few boxes out of my old apartment. It's an easy move, but I'm so grateful for their help. My parents told me I could keep or sell whatever furniture won't fit in my studio. So, I ended up selling a few pieces and used the money to pay for my move-in fee and to buy a smaller couch that has already been delivered to my new studio. As the guys are moving things over, I clean my old apartment.

I text them when I'm done. I leave my keys on the counter and take one last look at my first city apartment. So much has happened in the last six months. I walk out of this apartment for the last time and get into Vin's car. At my studio, we order pizza, and I get a six-pack of beer for James and Vin. I want to do something nice for them helping me.

After they leave, I spend the rest of the evening setting up my new home. It's late when I finish, but as I sit on my couch, ready to watch TV, I'm happy and already feel at home. I absolutely love my studio. Everything turned out perfect. I still can't believe I'm now living one block away from Michigan Avenue. I'm actually living my entire dream. I choose the next episode of *The Office*, and I remember it's Jim and Pam's wedding episode. This is going to be a good one to watch!

TWENTY

It's true what people say: Summertime in Chicago is everything. The city is beautiful and buzzing. The lake is now a turquoise blue and the skyline sparkles in the sunshine. People are out early every morning to capture the best of the day. Most days, as soon as my alarm goes off, I'm up and getting ready to go. I can now walk to work, and I find my morning walks are a pretty way to start my day.

I love people-watching: the waitstaff at restaurants outside preparing the patio cafés, opening the table umbrellas and adjusting the chairs for the eleven-to-one lunch rush. The early-rising tourists, coffee in hand, saunters the city to take in the sites, peer through shop windows, and gaze up at the tall buildings. The fancy ladies from the Gold Coast promenade the sidewalk with their little dogs, who by the way, are already dressed to the nines with full makeup and hair done. Then, there are people like me who enjoy a stroll to work and absorb the fresh early morning air. It gives me such a happy rush every morning. This is living life in the city.

Things are back on track for me. I'm back to blogging, and I've started talking to a group of people on social media who all live in the city. It's so cool because there is such a mix of people ranging from young girls like me just starting out in the city to more established girls, and guys as well, who work in a variety of fields. Since moving into my new apartment, I have gone to a few social meetups, and I have met a few new friends from social media.

I met one of the girls who I chat with regularly, and she is planning a girls' night after work. She's a little older than me and has lived in the city most of her life. I really like her. She has seen and done so much in the city. I love listening to all her stories. She has invited me and a few other girls, who I haven't met yet, to join her for drinks at *The Peninsula Hotel*. It is probably one of the nicest hotels in Chicago, and since I'm obsessed with hotels, I'm excited to meet her there for drinks.

It's four-thirty on Thursday, and tonight is the girls' night at *The Peninsula*. I'm wrapping up for the day so I can leave right at five, and my instant messenger pops up. It's Vin with his usual, *Yo*.

Sigh. I get up from my desk to head to his office.

"Can you shut the door." Every time he says something like this I can never tell what our conversation is going to be like.

"What's up?"

"I just want to talk to you about your position and all the things you have been doing over the last few months. You've taken on a lot more tasks and responsibilities since you started here. It's not fair that you are still only making an entry-level wage. So, I'm going to change your title from Receptionist to Executive Assistant and Office Coordinator. You've done so much since you've been here, and you work really hard. Starting next paycheck, I'm going to raise your salary by five thousand dollars."

"Really! Oh wow! Thank you! Thank you so much. I really, really appreciate it."

"Well, you deserve it, and like I said, you work really hard and make all our lives so much easier."

I didn't care that it just started to rain as I left the office. I'm thrilled. This extra money every month is going to help me so much. First things first though. I need to pay off a sizable chunk of my credit card. My city living is getting a little out of hand, and I need to get better at managing my going-out expenses. I put my umbrella up and head down Michigan Avenue toward *The Peninsula*.

I should have rethought my decision to walk because I'm pretty soaked by the time I get to the hotel. My hair is frizzy from the rain, and it's not the way I want to meet a group of new girls for the first time. I walk in and take a moment to figure out where I'm going. The concierge tells me to take the elevator up to the main lobby, so I do. When the doors open, I walk into a grand and beautiful hallway. The front desk is right in front of me and to the right is an elegant dining area. I ask an employee where I can find *The Bar*, and she directs me to around the corner.

I walk into a somewhat dark but cozy bar. There is a small bar to the left with a few seats, and the rest of the room is filled with comfy-looking chairs and couches. There is a grand fireplace, and I think how inviting it would be during the winter. I see my new friend waving to me, and I head over to her.

"Hi, Leah!" I look to the other girls sitting with her, and I give a smile.

"Heya, let me introduce you to everyone," I say hello and take a seat in the empty chair they saved for me.

"Sorry, I'm such a mess. I didn't realize how much it was really raining."

"You're fine. Did you want to order a drink?" Leah hands me a cocktail menu.

"Oh, yes, thanks." A waitress quickly comes over and takes my order.

I look around at the bar. "It's so cozy in here. I really like this hotel. It's beautiful.

"Yep, it is. If it wasn't raining, I wanted us to sit outside at *Shanghai Terrace*. It's literally a garden terrace that overlooks Michigan Avenue, and it's gorgeous. The drinks are really delicious too."

"Wow, that sounds so nice. I didn't even know they had a terrace here. I will have to go."

"Yep. So. How's the new apartment and the blog going?"

"The blog is fun, I enjoy working on it. The apartment is great. I love the location, and I'm okay with living in a studio. It's a nice size, and I have a big closet and bathroom. I didn't even have a closet in my last place."

"Are you serious? Is that even legal?"

"I'm not sure, but I was able to get out of my lease pretty easily. So, tell me about yourselves. I would love to hear more about you guys."

All the girls work in a variety of jobs from freelancing to PR and marketing. I find myself clicking with Leah and this girl Mary. All the girls are super nice and welcoming. Before we leave for the evening, we make plans to have cocktails at a few other places in the city. I want to try out new places, and I'm excited to meet up with them again.

It's not yet dark when we all leave *The Peninsula Hotel*. Since I live so close now, and it is still somewhat light outside, I decided to just walk home. Something I would have never done a few months ago. The rain has since stopped, and the sidewalks along Michigan Avenue have a pretty glow. It's turned out to be a lovely summer evening. The tourists are enjoying an evening stroll with ice cream or a Starbucks frappe. On my walk home, I watch as couples holding hands are either heading to or from dinner. Some girls have been shopping after work and carry their shopping bags in the crook of their arms. As I enter through my apartment door to my new little home, Gracie comes to greet me. She seems just as happy as I am to be here.

A few days later, I take a break from work to scroll through my social media feed. I see a post from a restaurant that I recently started to follow called *Sunda*. It's an Asian fusion restaurant, super trendy, and the food looks amazing. The post simply says, *Follow us, comment, and like this post for a chance to win a private dinner with our chef. Must be free to attend tonight.* I'm free tonight so, of course, I enter the contest. I return to my work, and I don't think much of it for the rest of the day.

Toward the end of the day, I receive a private message, still not thinking much about the contest, and open to see it is from *Sunda*. I've won two seats for the dinner tonight. They ask if I'm able to attend tonight and I can only bring one guest. I sit back in my chair, staring at my phone for a second because I can't believe that I have won. I check to make sure this is from the actual *Sunda* account and not a joke or spam. It's not. I've never won anything like this before.

Okay, so now, who should I bring? I can bring one of the girls, but how do I choose? I don't want anyone to feel left out. Maybe James? However, I know deep down inside who I want to ask, but should I? I would obviously talk about this experience on my blog. It would be a fun post. Would people ask who I took as my guest? No, probably not. Who's going to ask that, and why do I even care? Maybe someone in the office would ask, but I think only Jillian reads my blog. Okay, yep, I'm going to ask him.

I walk over to Vin's office. I see that he is busy. His door is open, so I just knock and stand in the doorway. He looks up.

"What's up?"

"Oh, nothing too much. Well, I'm wondering if you have plans tonight? I just won this really cool free dinner at *Sunda*. I'm wondering if you want to come with me?"

I can tell he's thinking about it. "What time?"

"I think it starts at seven."

"Okay, so how did you win this?"

"*Sunda* had a post to like, follow, and comment and so I did. I wasn't thinking much about it, so I just checked my account, and there was a private message from them."

"Wow, that's pretty cool."

"Yeah, it is, it sounds fun, and it's a free dinner. I've heard of *Sunda*, and I've wanted to check it out."

"I've never been either. I'm free, I'll go with you."

I give him a wide smile. "Cool."

"Well, I've got to get some work done then."

"Okay, I will go home and get ready, and I will meet you just before seven at *Sunda*."

"Yeah. Cool. I have a lot of work to do, so I will just meet you there."

"Okay, see you later then."

I stop by a few stores on my way home to find something cute to wear for tonight's dinner. I might want to take photos for my blog, so I want to make sure I look nice. I pop into Forever 21 to see what they have. They usually have cute dresses and for super cheap, so it's worth taking a look.

I leave the store with a simple blue dress after trying on half a dozen things. I look at my phone, and it's almost six. Yikes! I better walk home fast. I don't have much time to get ready and walk all the way over to *Sunda*. It's hot outside, so I don't want to rush and be all sweaty for dinner. I walk into my apartment at six-ten. I have about thirty minutes to freshen up, fix my hair, touch up makeup, and leave again. At least I have something to wear. I rush around, and at six forty-five, I'm ready to go. I give Gracie a treat, grab my key card, and run out of my apartment.

I end up having to walk fast, and I make it to *Sunda* right at seven. I check with the host and tell her I have won the dinner for tonight, and I give her my name. Then Vin walks up behind me. The host leads us through the restaurant and up the stairs to an open room. There is a long table, and in front of it, a chef is prepping it for dinner. We are in a private area of the restaurant. I had no idea it was going to be like this. I also notice that Vin and I are right now the only ones up here.

The host tells us someone will be by shortly to get our drink order and the rest of the parties should be joining us in a few minutes. Within a few minutes, another couple joins us and sits down across from us. They are an older couple and are friendly. By the questions they are asking, they think that Vin and I are a couple.

A server approaches and asks if we would like to start with a drink. He suggests a few cocktails, and I order something with mango. Vin orders a Jack and Coke. Our drinks arrive, however, no one else has joined our table. The four of us start some small talk as we wait for the server to return. He returns again with the chef who has finished prepping.

"Hello. Good evening guys. Thanks for coming. I'm Chef Jesse. We were going to have another larger party join us this evening, however, they have just canceled with us. So, it's just going to be the four of you this evening. This will give you a chance to have an intimate dinner and explore our menu here at *Sunda*."

Wow. This is a private dinner, in a private room, and now everything is going to be prepared just for us.

I look over at Vin. "How fun is this going to be!"

"Pretty cool. I'm impressed. I've never done anything like this."

I literally can't go over each course we have. There are so many, and each one is better than the last. Everything we try is amazing. Chef Jesse takes his time with everything he cooks and prepares for us. Along with personally serving each course to us, while we eat, he explains how everything is cooked and prepared. You can tell he's passionate about his food. Throughout the evening, he laughs and jokes and is having fun right along with us. It's time for dessert, which must have been at least our eighth course. I'm so full. I've surprised myself, because I actually try everything Chef Jesse has served, including things that were raw and somewhat slimy.

"So good right?" I give a Vin nod.

"So good. I can't believe that we got to do all this. Such an amazing night."

"I know! I really had no idea it would be like this. I just figured we would get a free meal or try a tasting menu or something."

After our dessert course, we thank Chef Jesse over and over for such an amazing meal and a memorable night. We leave both Chef Jesse and our server a gracious tip, say goodbye to the older couple. We walk out into a warm summer night.

"I absolutely love when the weather is like this. It's a perfect summer night."

"I can walk you home if you would like?"

"Okay, yeah, thank you. Let's definitely walk since it's such a nice evening."

We head in the direction of my apartment chatting the whole time about the evening. Although, I've had a great night with Vin something is brewing inside me. I just can't let it go. I need to ask him. Not letting go of what's on my mind is something I often do, and I think it can sometimes be one of my worst qualities.

I don't have much time to ask since we are about five minutes from my apartment building. While Vin is talking about something else, I just let it come pouring out.

"What happened with you and Natalie on Memorial Day weekend?"

He doesn't say anything at first. I can tell he is trying to think about what happened that night.

"You know, the night we all met at *RPM*."

"Oh, that night. Oh, I think we just went to Leg Room, had a few drinks, and that was about it."

"So, nothing happened between you and her."

"No, nothing happened. Why are you asking this now? Why do you want to know?" Vin stops abruptly in the middle of the sidewalk and looks at me.

"I don't know. I just know that she likes you, you know."

"So, I've heard. But you seem to bring her up way more than I do. She's a very nice girl, but I'm just not into dating anyone right now. I think I've told you this already. I was dating my last girlfriend for a long time, and it's just not something I'm looking for right now."

I look down at the ground. "Oh right. Of course. I'm sorry for bringing it up to you again. I know, it's not my business who you date. It's just that I enjoy your company. You've helped me so much, and you have helped me become more comfortable with being on my own in the city. I'm not sure I'm ready for that to change just yet."

"Well, I have fun with you too. Like tonight. Tonight, was so much fun. When I like someone, I promise you, you will be one of the first to know."

I feel better hearing that. "Okay. That's a deal then. I did have a lot of fun tonight, thank you for going with me."

"Thanks for asking me. It was an amazing dinner."

At this point, we are in front of my building, and I give him a quick hug.

"Also, thank you for walking me home."

"Always."

"Okay. Well, see you in the morning."

I look back at him as I open the door to my building. He gives me a quick wave and starts walking away.

TWENTY-ONE

J uly is hot. The city is sizzling. The air doesn't move. I'm sticky every morning when I walk to work. I have switched from a hot coffee to an iced coffee most mornings. Feeling hot from my walk this morning, I sit down at my desk and take a few sips of my iced coffee, waiting to cool off a bit. Mark comes busting through the front glass doors. He's here early this morning. I wonder what could be going on? However, instead of walking into the model side, he comes right over to my desk. Oh geez, what could he possibly want from me?

"Kelly. My publicist called me today with good news." Really? He has a publicist?

"I entered into a contest for *Esquire Magazine's* "Best Dressed Man of the Year," and I'm going to be on *The Today Show* next week. You're looking at the next Best Dressed Man of the Year. You can tell all your girlfriends that you work for me."

"Wow! That's really . . . great! We'll have to watch when you're on."

"Cool. Well, I was wondering if you could do me a huge favor?" Oh no.

"Okay, what's that?" I look up and give him a big smile.

"I would like you, as my favorite assistant, to send over some flowers to Kathie Lee."

"Kathie Lee Gifford? Whatever for?"

"Hoda and Kathie are hosting the contest on the show. I met her a few years ago in New York. I want to send her some flowers to let her know I'm one of the contestants. I'm sure she'll remember me. I'll email you the details."

I roll my eyes as Mark heads back to his office. He is unreal. I wish he would spend more time helping the models than working on his fame. Later in the afternoon, he sends me all the details. I spend most of the afternoon looking for the perfect flowers for Kathie Lee. At least he gave me his credit card. Never a dull moment with Mark. Of course, I tell the whole office that Mark is going to be on *The Today Show*, and honestly, we can't wait to watch it. I can only imagine what his segment will be like.

It's still so hot by the weekend. Kourtney has a pool and has invited Amy and me over to lay out and swim for a few hours. Her building is right next to an exclusive club, East Bank Club, where Oprah used to go. Anytime you hear about East Bank Club, someone will always say, did you know that's where Oprah hung out? Chicago is very proud to have had Oprah for so long and really who wouldn't be?

Kourtney's place is beautiful. Everything looks brand new, and the rooftop is vast with a huge pool, plenty of lounge chairs to lay out on, and a large garden area. There are fire pits with groups of couches surrounding them and a few grills scattered nearby.

"Wow! Kourt, this place is amazing! It's so nice up here. I can't believe you live here."

"I know! It's a million times nicer than our old place in New York. Did I already tell you that?"

Kourtney talks a lot about New York City. She compares everything to New York. She loves New York, and I can tell she misses it.

"Yep. Do you think you'll go back to New York?"

"I think eventually. But right now, my fiancé has such a good job here so we will be here for a while I guess."

"Well, at least you get to live in this really amazing place!"

We grab three chairs together right next to the pool and spread out our towels. This is seriously so nice. I could literally do this every weekend. We lay out for the next few hours. I love feeling the sunshine, even when it's hot. The pool is perfect. We enjoy a few mimosas, then take a quick dip to cool off, and lay out again to get more sun.

"So, what are your plans for this evening? I think Amy and I are going with the guys to a sushi spot that's kind of a hidden gem. It's in the Belden Stratford. I think it's called *Naoki*. Have you heard of it?"

"No, but I looked at apartments there. That sounds cool. I had no idea that was even in there."

"Yeah, you're welcome to come with us. See, you need to start dating someone so you can come on dates with us all the time."

"Well, thank you. I would go, but I'm meeting Vin and James at a BBQ place in Wicker Park called *Smoke Daddy*. I haven't really been over to that area, so I think we will walk around for a bit and then go eat."

"So, do you hang out with them a lot?"

"Well, I've hung out James quite a bit, and sometimes Vin joins us."

"What do you think of Vin?"

"I enjoy spending time with him. He's fun to hang with, and he has helped me to become way more comfortable with living in the city."

"Oh, so you guys are pretty close then, huh? Well, I still think that you should let me hook you up with one of my fiancé's coworkers. You definitely don't want to get involved like that with your boss. What if you guys break up? That could totally ruin your job."

"Well, it's really not like that, we're just good friends."

"Oh, okay" She gives me a questioning look.

"Well, if you want to meet some of my fiancé friends, let me know. I think it would be great."

"I will for sure. I just feel like I want to have fun right now. I'm still pretty new to the city, and I'm enjoying just exploring and figuring things out."

"Totally, Kelly." Amy interjects. "Don't let Kourtney push you. There's no rush." She looks over to Kourtney and playfully sticks out her tongue.

I leave Kourtney's around four o'clock. Vin is coming by around six to pick me up. This gives me plenty of time to shower and to get ready. I try not to think about my conversation with Kourtney and Amy. I know what I'm doing is harmless. For some reason, they just think it's inappropriate that I hang out with Vin. I think they are wrong. He's such a nice guy, and they hardly know him like I do.

I put on a pair of shorts and a cute tank. It's still hot outside. I add a pair of wedges, and I'm ready. Just after six, I get a text from Vin saying that he is downstairs.

"Hi!"

"Hey, you look tan."

"Yeah, a little red maybe, I spent the day at Kourtney's pool."

"How was that?"

"Really fun. She lives in a beautiful building that has an amazing rooftop with a pool. I've never been to a building like that before."

"Cool. Are you hungry? James is going to meet us over there."

"Yep, I'm pretty hungry."

Wicker Park is very different from Downtown, Lincoln Park, and Lakeview. It's a little grungier and has a different vibe. Vin told me he used to live in Wicker Park before moving to downtown, and he loves the area.

"It's very artsy and unique. I'm excited to see what it's like."

"Yeah. I will show you all my favorite spots."

We walk first to *Smoke Daddy* and put our name on the waiting list. They tell us it's going to be about a one-hour wait for the patio. That gives us plenty of time to walk around for a bit. We meet up with James and walk around Division Street and over to Damen and Milwaukee Avenue so I can see what the neighborhood is like. Vin points out all the spots he used to hang at and tells us a few stories about starting his agency in Wicker Park.

"Do you see this wall here?" Vin points to the wall we are walking by on Damen Avenue.

"Yep. What is it?"

"It's often painted with different murals. But, behind this door right here, there's kind of hidden bar called *The Violet Hour*. This bar is really a hidden gem. It's a speakeasy, but it also reminds you of something out of 'Alice in Wonderland.'"

"Oh, that's really cool. I'm adding it to my list for sure. I would love to see what's inside. What a cool concept. You would never know that place was there."

"Yep. It's a pretty cool spot."

We're starting to get hungry, and we head back to the restaurant. We wait another ten minutes or so, and our table on the patio is ready. The host seats us at a table along the street. Above us are lots of twinkly lights. It's twilight, so the sky is somewhat light, but it's still pretty. Dining on a patio at nighttime has become one of my favorite things to do. I want to sit outside as much as I possibly can.

The food is awesome at *Smoke Daddy*. I order my usual pulled pork with coleslaw that comes with a side of their sweet BBQ sauce. I end up eating most of my sandwich. We all order a second round of drinks, so we can sit and enjoy the evening air. Vin drops me off a few hours later, just after ten. I'm exhausted from all the sun. It was a full day. I literally crawl into bed a few minutes later and fall fast asleep.

Last night, Vin asked if I wanted to meet up and explore the *Chicago Riverwalk*. He has been there a few evenings this summer for drinks with his friends since he lives so close in Marina City. I haven't really been over there to hang out yet, but I heard it's one of best places to go during the summer.

I meet him over near his apartment on Sunday afternoon, and we walk down the stairs to the *Riverwalk*. It's a beautiful day, and it is packed. Couples strolling into bars. People walking their dogs or riding their bikes. Some are partying and playing music on boats docked along the river.

We walk up and down the *Riverwalk* first so I can see all the spots to hang out. I love the Tiki bar that's close to Navy Pier, but after walking back, we end up ordering a glass of wine at *City Winery*. We find a seat near the steps by the river to relax and enjoy our glass of wine and watch the boats sail by. We sit in silence for a while to take in this pretty day and watch all the happenings around us.

"This is so nice. I could totally sit here all day, but I'm also getting a little hungry. Are you?"

"Yeah. I definitely need to eat something if I'm going to drink any more wine. Kourtney told me yesterday about this restaurant that I think might be kind of close by. Let's see, I think it's called *Hampton Social*. Do you want to go check it out?"

"Sure, if you want to."

"I guess the restaurant makes you feel like you're hanging out in the Hamptons or something. It has to be walkable from the *Riverwalk*."

Vin looks it up on his phone. "Yeah, it is. Not too far at all. Looks good. Let's go."

"Okay, one second. Kourtney also told me about this app called *OpenTable*. You can make reservations to restaurants all over the city and get points toward gift cards. I just downloaded it yesterday, and I want to see if I can make a reservation."

I open the app and search for the restaurant. "Perfect. They have a reservation for three-thirty."

"Great. Book it."

We finish our wine and head over to *Hampton Social*. Kourtney had described the restaurant exactly how it looks. We are lucky to get a table by the open windows. I love the dècor in here. Everything is white and blue and has a very nautical East Coast beach vibe.

"Have you ever been to the Hamptons?"

"No. Have you?"

"No, but I really want to someday. Oh, you know what, I'll be right back. I want to get a photo of that *Rosé All Day* sign on the wall before someone sits here."

We split a pizza and order two glasses of their rosé of the day. It is refreshing on a hot summer day. It's after five when we leave the restaurant. I'm feeling pretty happy from both the wine and the weekend out in the sun. Summer weekends in Chicago are literally the best. I'm sad for the day to be winding down.

"I know we have been out most of the day, but do you want to do one more thing before you go home?"

"Okay, sure. What's that?"

"I looked up something for us to do at a restaurant. I wanted to see if anything is going on today."

"Okay, tell me!"

"Over in *Millennium Park*, at the *Pritzker Pavilion*, they have either a concert or a movie during the evening on certain days of the week. Tonight, they have a free concert. It starts in a little while. We could walk over there and check it out. We don't have to stay for the whole thing."

"Ooh yes! Let's go! I've wanted to go to a movie in the park, but a concert sounds really fun too!"

We find seats in the pavilion and watch the orchestra set up. I check out the people around us who brought food and drinks and set down blankets in the picnic area on the lawn behind us.

I whisper to Vin. "We should have brought some wine with us. I didn't know you could bring drinks in here."

"I didn't know either. I have never watched a movie or been to a concert here before."

"For living in the city for so long, you really haven't done too much." I kid with him.

"I've haven't really met anyone who likes to do things like this."

I give Vin a smile. He is right. I haven't known anyone who likes to do these things either.

The orchestra begins to play, and I'm totally mesmerized. Its' sound is so beautiful, and as the sun goes down, the lights from high-rises around us get brighter, and the whole city is glowing. It's magical. I feel so content to be sitting here in the middle of this amazing city listening to music.

Today is the day that Mark is on *The Today Show*. The whole office crams into the conference room to watch his segment. Five guys are the finalists, and they each have to convince Kathie Lee and Hoda and the editor of *Esquire Magazine* who is the best-dressed man in America.

The three judges will then vote on the winner, which will be at the end of the segment. Mark comes on TV and we all cheer. We might tease him in the office as to how much of a big shot he thinks he is, but at the end of the day, you have to be proud of him for getting this far. I mean, he is on *The Today Show*. Kathie Lee introduces each one of the finalists who show off their personal style and convince the judges why they are the best-dressed man in America.

Mark is the second to last to show his stuff, and he actually does really well. The last guy is up, and they cut to commercial. When the show comes back to air, they have recap the news, recap the weather, and go to commercial again. Finally, the show opens again, and it's time to announce the winner. Mark doesn't win first place, unfortunately, but comes in second. He must be bummed. So, our excitement for the day is over, we turn off the TV, and get back to work.

Two days later, Mark is back from his New York trip.

"Hey! How was it? We all watched you, and we all thought you did really great!"

"Oh. Thanks. I was a little bummed that I didn't win, but it was fun. It was a fantastic opportunity and looks really good on my resume."

"Okay, you have to tell me all about behind the scenes. I'm always really interested in that stuff."

He tells me what it's like to be on *The Today Show*, and it does sound really cool.

"So. Maybe you want to do me another favor?"

"Okay, sure."

"The day I was on the show, Kerry Washington was also on. We hung out in the green room for a bit, and she is really cool. Like really, really cool."

"Really? Wow! That is cool. I really like her!"

"Yeah. We hit it off really well. So, I was wondering if you could figure out who her people are and send her some flowers from me?"

He has a big grin, but I laugh and shake my head. "She married you know, with kids!"

He keeps that grin on his face and heads back to his office. It's never a dull moment, always the same Mark.

TWENTY-TWO

I get up early this morning so I can spend a little more time on my hair and makeup. This evening Jillian and I are both invited to an event at Swarovski on Michigan Avenue. They are launching a new line, and I was invited along with a few other Chicago bloggers to cover it.

It's my first invite to cover an event for my blog, and this time I'm definitely wearing a little black dress and a pair of black heels. I felt so out of place last time. Maybe it's silly to feel this way, but I want to fit in with the rest of the bloggers. I want others to know I'm serious about my blog. As I walk into the office, I get a few weird looks from some of the guys.

"Hmmm good morning. So, why are you so dressed up today?"

"Well, James. Jillian and I got invited to cover an event tonight at Swarovski."

"Ohhh, so fancy!"

"I'm pretty excited since it's my first official event that I have been asked to cover."

"Well, that's cool. I'm excited for you."

I notice that as everyone walks in, they give me a double take. Mark comes busting through the glass doors as always in his standard outfit of jeans, vest, and Prada bag. He takes off his sunglasses and looks at me.

"You have a hot date tonight or something?"

"No, I'm going to an event after work."

He gives me a strange look as to whether it is the truth or not. "Hmm cool."

Vin walks in and gives me a big smile. "You look nice."

I can feel myself instantly getting red. I give Vin a half smile and try to focus on the emails in my inbox. I have a message from Leah. She is planning a girls' night next week at a place called *Cindy's* and asks if I'm free. I have no idea where that is, but I tell her I'm in. I open a new tab in my browser and type in *Cindy's Chicago*. I see that it's a rooftop bar and restaurant at the *Chicago Athletic Association Hotel*. I look through the images. The rooftop is gorgeous and has an amazing view of all of *Millennium Park* and the lake. I haven't been to a rooftop yet, and I'm so excited to go.

Jillian and I hang out together in the office after work. We don't have to be at the event until six. I haven't spent much time with Jillian lately, so it's nice to spend some quality time with her. She's more open and social with me then she used to be.

Just before six, we leave the office and head toward Swarovski. We walk in and see it's decorated so beautifully. Their newest collection is out on displays with giant sparkling crystals hanging everywhere you look. White and blue balloons float in the air all around the store. Each employee is wearing pieces from the collection, and each piece is so gorgeous. There are a lot of large sapphire and white crystals in this collection.

We are offered a glass of champagne and look around at each piece in the collection. I have my eye on a pair of gorgeous sapphire drop earrings. As I'm browsing similar earrings, Jillian grabs my arm.

"Oh my gosh, the fashion editor of *Runway Magazine* is here!" She excited, and I turn around to look.

If I'm going to be honest, I have no idea who the fashion editor of *Runway Magazine* is. I follow Jillian to where the editor is standing. She is surrounded by girls asking her questions. They all seem to be gushing at the chance to talk to her. She's obviously a big deal, and I feel kind of dumb that I don't know who she is.

The editor is quickly whisked away by her assistant, so they can take photos and wrap up what they need for their article. I made a mental note to look up how they covered this event. I want to get some tips from a major magazine.

This event isn't as crowded as the Kenneth Cole event, so we just hang around a little while longer and mingle with some of the other bloggers and a few PR people.

As some of the event goers are leaving, the host at the front of the store is handing out little blue bags as a thank you for coming. We peruse the store one more time to make sure we have enough photos then head out. We thank the host as she hands us our gift bag. I have never received a gift bag from an event, and I can't wait to see what's inside.

"What did you think of your first official event?"

"It was good. Not as exciting as the first one, but a fun first event to cover for my blog. I'm just happy I was invited."

"Good. Well, it's only just after seven, so do you want to go to *RL* since it's on our way home. You have wanted to go there."

"Oh, yeah! Okay, let's do that. Great idea Jillian."

RL is just what I expected. The restaurant is very sophisticated and timeless. The host seats us in a cozy booth. There are pictures everywhere along the walls. I pick up the menu, and I see the grilled cheese and tomato soup that Jillian told me about. It's one of my favorite comfort food in the fall and winter.

"So, what are you going to get. The burger here is really good. Do you also want to get a glass of wine?"

"Sure. Why not? Well, I do love grilled cheese and tomato soup, but it just seems too hot for that, so, I will go with the burger if that is what you are having."

The waiter brings us a basket of bread, and we order two glass of white wine and two burgers.

"How's work going for you lately? I hope hiring another person has helped you."

"Yeah, it's been a huge help. I can focus more on strategy. Sam is doing more of the writing and social media. I feel much less stressed."

"That's good. I feel like I've gotten better at doing all the accounting. The last few months have been so busy. Anyway, what do you think is in this gift bag? Is that normal?"

"No, not really, but let's open them."

"Okay."

I undo the ribbon and open the bag. Inside is a thank you card from the store manager and a little blue box. Inside the box is a pair of round studs filled with mini crystals. They are so simple, yet so pretty. I love them.

"Wow, what a beautiful gift!"

"Yes, I didn't think it would be as nice as this. Any gift is usually something promotional from the store."

"Well, these will be perfect for my post. I can wear the earrings with a cute outfit and show how to style them for every day and write all about the event."

"That's a fun idea. I'm asked just to strictly write about the event, which gets kind of boring."

"Well, maybe you can spice it up a bit. Tell people how to style some of the pieces or something."

"Yeah, maybe."

The server comes over with two huge burgers. "Wow, there's no way I can eat all of this."

I cut my burger in half. I can save the other half for dinner tomorrow. I take a big bite, and Jillian is right, the burger is good.

"What do you think?"

"It's great. I really like this place, it's so nice."

"Yeah, it's kind of a staple here in Chicago and a good place to come all year around."

After dinner, we slowly walk together toward Delaware, where we now always part ways and go in our opposite directions.

"I can't believe you live a few streets away now. Isn't it crazy how things work out? You thought you would never be able to afford to live around here."

"I know, it's crazy! So much has changed in the last few months.

I had a few bumps in the beginning, but things are really working out now."

"You've definitely come along way, and you're totally more of a city girl now. You were kind of a confused mess in the beginning. You always looked so nervous."

"I did."

"Yeah, but that's okay, you got there in the end."

"Yep, I'm getting there, things are definitely working out great."

TWENTY-THREE

S adly, for me, summer is slowly coming to an end. Even though the days are still warm, the weather cools down in the evenings, and the leaves are starting to change.

Transitioning a wardrobe into a new season can sometimes be difficult. It's hard to know how to dress, what to wear. I think layering is always the best option. I'm wearing a pair of cropped black pants, a silky tank top, and my favorite jean jacket that I've had for forever. It's a good in-between summer and fall look and looks cute enough to meet up with the girls for cocktails at *Cindy*'s.

As I leave my building to walk outside, I wonder who Leah invited and if it would be the same girls from last time. I'm hoping Mary is coming again. I had fun with her and Leah last time. We are not meeting 'til around six, so I have plenty of time to meet the girls. I take my time to wander in and out of a few stores along Michigan Avenue.

Each store has exploded into fall fashion season. I browse through so many cute sweaters and jackets, but I don't have time to shop now. Maybe I will do a little shopping this weekend. I'm trying to be wise and use the extra money in my paycheck to pay down my credit card balance; however, I think shopping for a few fall staples is okay. I've been getting all my fashion style tips from Kourtney, and she says that you always need a few nice staple pieces each season.

I quickly hop on a bus going south-bound on Michigan Avenue. It's five minutes to six, and I walk into the Chicago Athletic Association and toward the elevator that goes up to the rooftop. The doors open, and I get into the elevator and hit the top-floor button to *Cindy*'s. When I arrive, the doors open again, right onto the rooftop.

I say hello to the host and tell her I'm meeting a friend. She gives me a friendly smile directs me to where Leah is seated. This time, I'm the first of the group to arrive, and I'm not soaking wet from the rain.

"Hiya!" She greets me as I sit down across from here.

"Hey, how are you?"

"Good, just been busy with work. Everything is going well, but this new freelance job makes me go through a lot of people to get things done. But, that's corporate life for you." As she finishes her sentence, we hear someone walking over and look up to see Mary is making her way over.

"Hey, guys. How are you? I haven't been here in a while."

"This is my first time here," I admit to her.

"Oh, it's great. The food, the cocktails, everything is great."

I glance over the menu. "Is anyone else joining us, Leah?"

"No, just the three of us tonight."

I'm okay with this. I really like the other girls, but smaller groups are more fun, and I really like the company of Leah and Mary. We each order a cocktail and chat for ages. They are just so cool because they know so much about everything in the city. They have seen and done so much, and they know all the newest spots. I wonder if, in a few years, I will be like them?

The server comes by, and we order another cocktail and decide to share the shellfish platter. However, our server doesn't come back with our cocktails. Instead a young man comes to our table with three of the same cocktails on a tray.

"Hi, Leah!"

"Oh, my gosh, hi!" She stands up to greet him as he hands

Mary and me our cocktails. "Ladies, this is Mike. He is the manager here at *Cindy's*."

"Hi, ladies, nice to meet you all. I saw that Leah was sitting over here, and I wanted to bring you one of our signature cocktails that will be on our new fall menu."

"Wow! Thank you so much."

"You're very welcome. I hope you enjoy. It was nice to meet you ladies and please feel free to come back and ask for me anytime."

"Okay, we will."

"Wow Leah, how nice of him." I take a sip of my cocktail. It is delicious, and he's right, it is perfect for fall.

"Yeah. I've known him for a while. I've been coming here quite a bit with my friends. He's a really nice guy."

Before our shellfish platter arrives, we all get up from our table to look at the view. I look out over the glass balcony. *Millennium Park* is right across from the hotel. The leaves are changing to bright yellow and orange colors throughout the park. The lake is beyond the park and is still blue even early in the evening. This view is stunningly exquisite, and I cannot help but take a few photos.

Our seafood arrives, and we eat and chat and enjoy the cocktails. Before we realize, it's just before nine, and we are all a little tipsy from our cocktails. We start to wrap up our evening since we all have work in the morning. It's been a fun night, and I'm bummed for it to end. I enjoy having a few girlfriends who you can spend having endless hours of conversation.

Before I head to bed, I send the girls all a text telling them I had a nice evening and hope to see them soon. I scroll through my social media and check my blog email. There's an email that was sent to me at four-thirty this afternoon.

Dear Kelly,

I hope this email finds you well. I recently met you at an event at Swarovski, and I wanted to invite you to our Chicago Fashion Week Runway Show. The event is on Friday, October 10th, at the main tent in Millennium Park. Your invite includes two VIP tickets to the show, an amazing goodie bag filled with tons of great products, and tickets to the after party at Underground nightclub.

Please see the attached materials to read about all the events we are hosting for Fashion Week.

We hope to see you there!

Kristy Vick

Director of Special Events

Please see attached

Wow! Wow! Wow! I cannot believe I got an invite to runway show. I didn't know there is a Chicago Fashion Week! I can't wait to tell Jillian about it tomorrow. I have no doubt she's invited to cover it as well. This is a huge highlight for me. I cannot believe that all my blogging and hard work is paying off. I'm so proud of myself for pushing to do something new. Jillian is right. It's still hard to believe that just nine months ago, I was this super shy girl moving to the city. I did not know anyone or anything about living here, and now I'm going to this special event.

Jillian is always in the office before me, so I leave a little earlier for work so I can tell her about the exciting news.

"Morning! I really have to tell you something."

"Morning, ah okay, what is it?"

"Well, last night I got an email with an invite to the "Chicago Fashion Week Runway Show." I have two free VIP tickets!"

"Cool! I'm going too. My editor told me about it a few days ago."

"Really? Yay! This is going to be so much fun. I need to read about the Chicago designers that are headlining so I know who to look for."

"It's all on the website, I can send it over to you."

"Okay, thank you! That would be great."

"Wait, Kelly. What's going on? Come over here." I hear Amy calling my name from the other side of the wall.

"Okay, be right there." I head over to tell her my news.

"So, tell me. What are you so excited about?"

"Well, I'm invited to Chicago Fashion Week! I have two VIP tickets for the event in October. It includes drinks and apps obviously, but also a huge gift bag and tickets to the after party at *Underground.*"

"How cool! So, who are you going to bring?"

"Well. Jillian is already going, and I would love all you guys to come. But, I only have one extra ticket."

"Well pick me. I definitely want to go with you." I knew Amy would want to go with me. She went to school for fashion design, and I know designing is her dream.

"Okay, you can, and we will just figure it out with the other girls."

"Figure what out?" Kourtney has just come into the office.

"Kelly is invited to Chicago Fashion Week. She has two VIP tickets to go to the event. She said I can be her guest, and we will figure out tickets for you and Natalie."

"Well, let's just buy VIP tickets and go. We can tell Mark that it's for work. You know researching models for events coming up."

"Oh my gosh, yeah. That's such a good idea. I will buy two tickets today."

"Perfect! I cannot believe we are all going to Chicago Fashion Week! I'm so excited!"

September is a busy month for fashion in Chicago. Vin let me leave for a few hours to attend a blogger's brunch at *Summer House Santa Monica* in Lincoln Park. It's a gorgeous place to host a brunch. The restaurant is bright and pretty and has an atrium roof. The decor makes me feel like it's summer every day. *Gilt City* is hosting the brunch to go over some fun and exclusive restaurants, spas, bars, and events that they are partnering with this fall season. They are hoping we will help spread the word or purchase some of the event or restaurant deals. I love the idea of getting a good deal to some of the best places in the city since it is expensive to go out all the time. As I look at the upcoming events, the fall wine tasting at *Eataly* really catches my eye.

Over the next week, I have an event to go to almost every night, and by Friday I'm exhausted! After work, I'm ready to go home and catch up on some TV or just watch a movie. I almost forgot that I promised my Mum that I will come home for the weekend. It's been awhile, so I'm taking the early train on Saturday morning.

After a weekend at home, I walk into work on Monday feeling

somewhat refreshed. I don't have much going on this week, and I'm looking forward to *not* having plans. I take a few minutes to enjoy my coffee and catch up on the Chicago news. I like to find out what new places are opening and read about the latest hot spots. I've downloaded this app on my iPhone called Checkli so I can add things to my growing list of all the places I want to try.

I see that today is officially the first day of fall. Summer is officially over. I absolutely love the summer. My first Chicago summer has been amazing. But I enjoy the fall season too, and I'm really looking forward to seeing how the city celebrates the holidays. I remember all the holiday lights and falling in love with the city that first time I visited all those years ago.

I look at my calendar to see which day is October 10th, the day of the Fashion Show. I have about two weeks until then. I look at tomorrow, it's the 23rd. The 23rd? Why does that date sound familiar? Do I have something planned for tomorrow? I look at the calendar on my phone and see that it's Vin's birthday. Oh no! I totally forgot! The office should really do something for him. I instantly send a message to James.

Hey!

Hi, what's up?

So, tomorrow is Vin's birthday. I almost forgot. Should I order lunch for him or something? What do you think?

Yeah, he would like that. Order pizza or something.

Okay, sounds good. I will also pick up a cake or dessert.

Okay, thanks.

I stop by Vin's office later in the day to see what he's been up to. "Hey, Hey! It's almost your birthday! Did you do anything fun to celebrate over the weekend?"

"I went out with the guys, but I didn't tell them it was my birthday."

"Really? Why not?"

"Guys don't do that."

"They don't? Hmm okay, well I hope you had fun anyway."

"Yeah, it was okay."

"So, what are you doing tomorrow night for your actual birthday?"

"I don't have plans."

"Oh. Well, we haven't hung out for a while. We can go to dinner or something if you like?"

He looks up at me. "I would really like that."

"Okay good. Me too."

Vin says it would be fun to go all out for his birthday dinner. I'm not sure what that means exactly, but he tells me he's been wanting to go out for a steak dinner for a while. He tells me *Mastro's* is his favorite and is best steak restaurant in Chicago. So, I make a reservation using *OpenTable* for seven.

Since it's still balmy for the end of September, I wear a silky green dress and my favorite pair of wedges. I bought this dress over the summer and haven't had a place to wear it. I grab a wrap just in case it gets chilly and head out the door. It's only a twenty-minute walk, but I decide to cab it there instead since it's almost seven and I don't want to be late.

I get out of the cab and walk toward *Mastro's*. Vin is already outside waiting for me. We greet each other with a quick hug and walk into the restaurant. A host takes us to a cozy booth in the bar area. The bar area is very dark and intimate. There is an older guy playing soft music on a grand piano, and the back of the bar is illuminated with bright, colorful lights, so all the bottles glow.

When Vin said he wanted to go all-out for his birthday, we really do, starting with the seafood tower. When the appetizer comes over, it's almost the size of our table. The seafood is fresh and delicious. I can never eat a whole steak by myself, so I tell Vin if he orders a steak I will have just a few pieces. We get the biggest filet Oscar-style, the twice baked potato, and a side of the lobster mac and cheese.

Even my lemon martini is over the top. I sip on it, which is served with dry ice and the whole shaker on the side. That is pretty much another martini and a half. After we finish our appetizer and drink half our first cocktails, we both start to relax a little more. I decide now is an appropriate time to ask Vin a few personal questions about himself. I feel like our conversation is flowing naturally in that direction. He has just shared with me his dreams for the future of the agency.

"I know that you are truly passionate about your company, and you should be, but do you have any other dreams or goals? Do you think about ever getting married or having kids?"

"Hmm, yeah, I guess so. I mean yes, I want to eventually get married. But it's not something I'm thinking about right now."

"Yeah, of course, you have a lot going on. I'm just wondering really."

Our food comes out. The steak and sides look unbelievably amazing. Our sides are brought out on a sizzling hot plate. The server asks if we need anything else. I cannot imagine needing anything else, and Vin and I continue our conversation.

"So, where are your parents and your sister? Do they celebrate your birthday with you?"

"Well, tonight my sister is working. She's a server at Weber Grill just down the street. My parents right now live in New York City. They also own a condo here in Chicago, so they come visit a few times a year."

"Wow, that's cool. Do they like New York?"

"My Mom does, she loves it. They also lived in Paris for ten years. They moved right after I finished high school."

"Really? That's amazing. I've never been to Paris."

"I've been a few times obviously to visit them. It's a nice city."

"Well, I'd love to go someday."

"Wait, you never went to Paris when you lived in London?"

"No, we only went to Ireland, Wales, and Portugal.

"Well, I moved around a lot as a kid."

"You did?"

"Yeah from Indiana to New York and Connecticut and then to Illinois."

"Wow, that is a lot of moving. After my parents decided to stay in the United States, we just stayed in the same place in the suburbs. They tried to move us a few times, but my brother and I thought where we lived was everything. Sometimes I wish now they would have made us move just to try somewhere else. I was very shy in school, and so the thought of moving to a new place terrified me. I've definitely come out of my shell a lot more over the years, and especially since I've moved to the city. I feel like a completely different person."

"You're definitely not the quiet girl you were when you started at the agency."

"Nope. I'm not." I put my fork down and my plate. "Everything was delicious, but I seriously can't eat another bite."

"Well, we can't *not* order the butter cake. It's the best dessert. Seriously, you have to try it."

"Okay, then. It's your birthday. Let's order the butter cake."

We order the butter cake, and Vin is so right. This cake just melts in your mouth, and it's so delicious. It would have been wrong to not order it.

We finish our dessert and drinks and ask for the bill. I get the check, and I look at the total. It's $198.68. Whoa. I want to pay for dinner, but including tip, over two hundred dollars is a little out of my price range. I just sit looking at the bill, trying to figure out how to pay.

"Kelly, you definitely don't have to pay for this. I got it. I picked this place."

"I really want to pay. I feel bad if you pay on your birthday."

"It's okay. I didn't expect you to pay for tonight. It's just nice to go out and have dinner with you."

I feel myself turning a little red. I feel awful that he is paying. Especially after he treated me on my birthday. "Well, only if you're really okay with it."

"Yes. My treat." He throws down his credit card.

For the fashion show, I shopped at H&M for the most perfect outfit. I'm wearing leather leggings, a long creamy-white tunic with an asymmetrical cut and lots of frilly layers. It's a little chilly out, so I'm also wearing my leather jacket. I have never bought a fun top like this one, and I love it. I feel very trendy and cool.

I arrive at the tent in *Millennium Park* just before six. Amy is already waiting for us. Ten minutes later all of us are together.

Everyone looks great, and we have really gone all out with our outfits for tonight. The tent is enormous. Huge spotlights shine all around the outside. I'm so excited to see what it looks like inside. We walk over to the VIP line and give our names. Once inside, the VIP section is crowded, and I can see that the runway area is currently roped off.

We find an area to hang out, and soon a waiter comes by with champagne. Fancy little appetizers are passed around to all the fashion-goers. We all sit in our little corner, watching everyone who walks in. Most of the people who enter our VIP area all seem to know each other and greet one another with that European double-kiss thing. It's definitely a scene and so much fun to watch.

We chat amongst ourselves and check out everyone's outfits. There is definitely a variety of styles from the simple black dress to outrageous, colorful outfits. Photographers walk around among the guests and ask to take photos of who they think is best dressed. At six forty-five, a voice on the microphone tells everyone to head into the main tent. Suddenly, everyone rushes to claim their seat. It's a little crazy, but we make it to our reserved seats in the second row. It's not a bad view for our first fashion show.

The woman on the microphone heads to the front and welcomes everyone to the show. She tells us a bit about the five Chicago designers who are presenting this evening, and the show will last about forty-five minutes to an hour. I smile at my friends. The announcer explains that after the show, the VIPs can exit at the left to receive their gift bag and tickets to the *Underground* after party. This is all exciting. None of us has ever done anything like this. During the show, we comment about what we love and don't love, and I try to take as many photos as I can for my blog.

There are lots of cheers for the five designers who come onto the runway at the show's end. It's then a mad rush for the exit. Luckily being on the left side, we easily get in line for our gift bags and after-party tickets. The gift bags are huge and filled with tons of goodies and products.

"Kelly, oh my gosh. That was so much fun! I'm so glad we all got to do this. I thought all the designers were amazing. I'm so glad I got to come with you. It was so inspiring."

"Yep. It was so much fun. I'm glad you enjoyed the show, Amy. The designers are all really great."

"Okay, so are we all going to *Underground*? What are we going to do with these huge bags?" Kourtney lifts her oversized gift bag up and down.

"Well, if you want, we can all leave them at my house. I live just down the street."

"Okay, yeah. That's a good idea. Let's leave them at Amy's."

We drop off our gift bags, then grab a cab to *Underground*. There's already a line outside, but we get in quickly with our VIP tickets.

We find an area to hang out. We dance together and enjoy the drinks that are comped from the fashion show. This is my first real city club experience, apart from our hosted event here a few months ago.

The music keeps getting louder and the club more crowded by the minute. Our area is no longer ours, so the only thing to do is to keep dancing. The crowd is wild with a similar kind of scene as the fashion show. We dance until we can't dance anymore. At this point, the music is so loud I can feel it vibrate throughout my whole body.

The club was such a rush, but after deciding we had enough of the dancing and the crowd, we head out just after midnight.

"Whoa, it's getting a little crazy in there. I can't believe how packed that place gets."

"I know. I've never been to a club like that before."

"Wait, Kelly. You haven't? Not even in college?"

"No, I really haven't."

"Wow. I used to sneak into clubs all the time in New York."

"Okay, you guys, we can stand out here talking about clubs all night, or we can go eat. I'm starving. All we really had tonight is the alcohol."

"It's after midnight. Are there any restaurants still serving food?"

"Actually Kell, there's a restaurant not too far from here called

Bijan's. It's open late so we can go there. They have good sandwiches, and the French onion soup is really good."

"Okay, let's go. I'm pretty hungry as well. Kourtney, Jillian are you going to come with."

"Sure, why not? The night is still young."

"And, you guys, it's been a night full of amazing firsts!"

TWENTY-FOUR

For Halloween, the entire office decides it would be fun if we dressed up. I convinced James to dress up with me and, of course, I suggest we dress up as Victoria and David Beckham. He's happy to go along with this because all he needs is a soccer outfit. I order a brown bob wig to match her famous haircut during her Spice Girl days. I wear the leather leggings that I bought for the fashion show, a long black fitted vest that buttons up in the front, and a pair of black heels. I look at my outfit in the mirror, and it looks pretty good.

I switch to my flats and carry my heels and purse to work. I'm getting a few looks from others on the sidewalk. Did people not know it was Halloween? I stop to pick up some Halloween-themed donuts, get my coffee, and head into the office. I walk through the glass doors of the office, and I hear Halloween music. I walk over to the team. Rather than being greeted by the usual morning face-in-the-computer zone, the team is sitting around the TV in the main room with bowls of candy around them.

"Hey James, what's going on?"

"Hey, Happy Halloween! Oh, you look great, like my soccer outfit? Ooh! You bought donuts, thanks!"

"You're welcome, so what are you guys doing?"

"We are setting up the Nintendo 64, we are going to have team races."

"It's not even nine in the morning yet."

"I know. We're just setting up now because races start at noon. Are you going to join us? Oh, we also have pizza coming for lunch."

"Okay, maybe."

I walk over to my desk and set my coffee down. I can't believe the office is this seriously excited about Halloween. I've never seen the team so alive this early in the morning. Candy wrappers are all over the office, so they are already hyped-up on sugar. It's going to be an interesting day.

The team does manage to get some work done in the morning, but as soon as it's noon they turn the music back up, and they are ready to go. The guys have set up a chart on the dry erase board to keep track of winners and who is racing whom. They are super serious about this.

Even Vin is into Halloween and is dressed like Michael Jackson. He also joins in on the racing. I watch for a little while from my desk and then go to see what the girls are doing. Jillian is just hanging out at her desk, dressed as a cute cat, and I ask her to come with me to hang at the models' side of the office. The three of them are dressed as cheerleaders.

"Oh my gosh, you guys all look super cute!"

"Thanks, Kell, love the Victoria Beckham."

"So, what are you guys doing over here?"

"Just hanging out. We're currently down the rabbit hole of makeup videos on YouTube and watching vlogs. You guys want to watch with us?"

"Yep, it's way better than getting involved with what the guys are doing."

"Cool. Grab two chairs and come sit. You guys want some champagne? You can make a mimosa?"

"Oh, yes please!"

Obviously, no one gets anything done the rest of the day. But, it's Friday, and it's nice to have a chill day. If Vin seems to be okay with it, then I am too. All of us girls, James, and a few others from the team leave work a little early for happy hour. Since we have been drinking most of the day, I'm home and in bed by nine. I didn't even check my phone at the end night. There was a message from Vin asking what I was doing. Oops! I feel so bad that I didn't see his text. I respond to him right away in the morning.

OMG! I'm so sorry! I fell asleep early last night, and I didn't even see your text. We were at happy hour for a while, and I needed to call it a night early.

No worries.

What are you doing today? Do you have any plans?

No.

Okay, do you want to meet up early afternoon?

Sure.

The weather had literally changed overnight. It's November 1st, and it's chilly. Knowing how Chicago weather goes, it's probably no longer fall, and winter is pretty much here. After relaxing all morning cozied up in my blanket and catching up on my shows, I text Vin again to see if wants to meet up. He responds yes and that he's just at home working.

Instead of texting back and forth, I decided to just call him to figure out what to do. Since it's chilly out, I don't really want to walk around the city. I dial Vin's number and let it ring. This is the first time I have called his phone, and he finally answers.

"Hey."

"Hey. I'm trying to think of something to do that is inside. I guess, we can see a movie. Or go eat somewhere, or even just go to a museum."

"A museum?"

"Yeah I haven't been to a museum in a long time, but it's just a thought."

"Okay, well what museum are you thinking? I haven't been to one in years either."

"Hmm, well I haven't been to the *Art Institute* in a long time. Could be fun, something different to do."

"Okay, give me thirty minutes and tell me where to meet you."

We plan to meet each other on Michigan Avenue at the Wrigley

Building so we can both walk to the *Art Institute* together. I get on the Michigan Avenue bus that will drop me off at the Wrigley Building. Although I usually enjoy my walk down Michigan Avenue, it's just too cold today, and I'm not used to the temperature change. I get off the bus and see him waiting for me in the open area by the Wrigley Building.

"Hey, can you believe how quickly the temperature changed? I couldn't walk down to meet you. I just had to get on the bus."

"It is chilly. Do you want to walk the rest of the way or take the bus?"

"Oh, it's not too far. I guess we can just walk."

It's cold, and the wind whips around us, but we walk the rest of the way to the *Art Institute* at Michigan Avenue and Adam Street. We go up the white steps of the Museum, pay for our tickets, and head into the lobby. It takes a few minutes to check out the map and decide what we want to see. We accomplished everything on our list. I especially love the Thorne Room, which has adorable miniature rooms and the painting *Love of Winter* by George Bellows. After spending almost two hours in the museum, we start to get hungry.

"Do you want to go eat at this great Thai restaurant that's kind of close to my apartment? It's the best Thai in the city. We can cab it there since it's chilly out."

"Okay, yeah that's sound great."

We leave the museum and take a cab to this little-hidden gem that I've never seen before. *Star of Siam* is just below Wabash on Illinois Street. The host seats us at a booth that we literally have to climb into, then he hands us two menus.

"I wouldn't usually tell you what to eat, but can I order for us. I promise you will like it."

"Okay, sure."

Vin's orders Massaman curry and the grounded basil chicken. The meals come quickly, and Vin is right, both dishes are delicious. It's the perfect thing to eat on a chilly fall day.

"Do you have any plans for this evening. Want to see a move or something?"

"No, I don't have plans. Let's look up some movies to see what's playing."

We have just enough time to make it to a movie that we have both been wanting to see. We grab two seats in the back row with a few minutes to spare before the movie starts.

"This has been a fun day," I whisper to Vin as the movie begin. He looks over at me and gives me a nod and taps the top of my hand.

On my way home, Vin and I stop by *676* for a glass of wine. We get a little table right by the window so we can look over Michigan Avenue. The buildings are lit up, and this view is always so pretty. I feel content and happy. We drink our wine and chat about the movie.

When I'm back in my apartment that evening, I think about the day. It has been a perfect Saturday, so perfect that I'm feeling so torn about how I should feel. I can't stop thinking about all the advice my friends have given me over the last few months. Whenever I start thinking about how much I enjoy my time with Vin, Kourtney's words replay in my head. Dating your boss is a bad idea, it could ruin your job. Even though Vin and I have spent time together alone, and it's always really nice, it's not like Vin really acts as though he likes me in that way.

He doesn't get too close to me when we are together, and our time together doesn't really feel like a date. If anything, he's one of my closest friends. For right now, I'm okay with that. However, after spending today with him, I know that I'm going to just stop being so concerned about what other people think.

TWENTY-FIVE

I t's the week of Thanksgiving, and we have off tomorrow, Thursday, and Friday. I'm going to my parents' house tomorrow and coming back sometime on Friday or Saturday morning. I don't want to leave little Gracie for longer than that. Also, this is a great weekend to shop, and I have never shopped the Thanksgiving sales on Michigan Avenue. So, that's something I'm looking forward to doing.

This evening, a few of us are going to a low-key bar for a few drinks before we head out of the city for the holiday weekend. Before I go out this evening, I desperately need to get some food and litter for Gracie before I leave her for a few days. It's such a pain to get cat litter. It's so heavy and not sold anywhere close to my apartment. Vin has offered to take me to the store after work so I can get what I need. Together, we walk over to his place to pick up his car.

"I've never been to a big Target in the city and, this might sound silly, but I'm kind of excited about this."

"You girls get excited about the weirdest things."

"Maybe, but it's Target. Everything is great at Target." He laughs at me as we walk inside.

"Okay, Vin, it's time to do some damage." I grab a cart, and we stroll around the aisles looking at everything. Before we know it, we have a lot of random things in our cart, and we head toward the checkout.

"See, this always happens. You can't ever leave Target and not spend at least fifty dollars on stuff you never knew you needed."

"Well, shopping with you is dangerous. I don't even know what's in this cart."

I give him a grin. I hand over my credit card to the cashier, and a few minutes later, we are back in the car, and on I-90 heading back to downtown.

"So, you better come with us tonight to get some drinks?"

"Maybe, but I feel like there is something I need to tell you." I look over at him. He looks nervous, and I'm wondering what could be so serious.

"Okay, sure. Of course. Is there something wrong?"

"No. Nothing is wrong. I just feel like I need to tell you something that's been on my mind for a while.

"Okay. Like what?" My heart starts beating faster, and now I'm getting nervous.

"I have a little bit of a crush on you."

Complete silence. I don't say anything. I don't even look at him. Instead, I turn and look out the window. It feels like a really long time before I finally answer and it's starting to get awkward.

"You do?"

"Well, what I meant to say was, I did have one. I just wanted you to know that I did have feelings for you, but I don't anymore."

"Wait, so you don't anymore?"

"I'm sorry. I shouldn't have said anything. I really don't want things now to be awkward between us, but I just thought you should know. Remember when I left your house after the movie? It's because I liked you, and I often get nervous to be around you. Whenever I walk with you or take you home, I get sad to leave you, so I just walk away. I've tried to not let you know my feelings because I'm your boss and I don't want to make you feel uncomfortable."

"So, you want me to know that you did have feelings for me. But that you don't anymore."

"I just thought you should know."

I don't know what else to say and, obviously, neither does he. We drive the rest of the way in total silence. He pulls the car up to my apartment building.

"Okay, well, thank you for driving me so I could get this stuff. I really appreciate it." I grab my bags, and cat litter, and get out of his car. "So, will I see you tonight?"

"Maybe."

I breathe in and give him a little sigh. "Well, I hope you come but if you don't have a good Thanksgiving. Hopefully, I'll see you this weekend when I get back from the 'burbs."

"Yeah, just text me or something."

"Okay, I will."

I feel terrible. I knew I had thrown him off, regardless if he still likes me or not. It was rude of me to not say anything. I shouldn't have sat there, and I knew I had hurt his feelings. I literally just froze, and I'm so mad at myself. Honestly, I didn't know how to respond to what he was saying, but I handled it terribly. Do I have feelings for him too? I suddenly feel so confused but, if I did, I have blown that chance now.

James told us to meet at the bar at eight. Although now, I don't feel like being social, I'm going just by chance that Vin will show up. I want to talk to him and fix things. I want to tell him in person that I'm sorry. I really don't want things to be weird the next time I see him. When I get to the bar, James and only a few of his friends are there. No Vin. By nine-thirty, I knew he wasn't coming.

"Hey Kelly, what's going on with you tonight. You've been really quiet. Is something wrong?"

"Well, I don't even know where to begin. I don't really want to talk about this with anyone, but I feel like I can trust you. Maybe you can give me some advice?"

"Okay, sure. What's going on?"

"Well, for the last few months I know that we have hung out with Vin outside of work. But, I've also spent quite a lot of time with just him. We always have a lot of fun together, and I really enjoy spending time with him. We have a lot in common. So then, after work today, he drove me to run some errands, and he told me he has feelings for me. I didn't say anything, so then he said, "Well I *used* to have feelings for you."

"Yikes! Kelly! Why didn't you say anything?"

"I don't know. I just froze. I honestly didn't know what to say or how to respond. I didn't want to say anything that would hurt his feelings. I don't know if I feel the same way, or if I'm afraid to feel the same way. So, I just said nothing."

"Well, I'm not surprised he told you. I kind of knew he has or had feelings for you?"

"Wait. What? James! You did?"

"Yeah. I mean he hasn't told me directly, but I just had a feeling. I could tell. I know you guys are hanging out because he would tell me and ask me if he should do this or that with you. Also, I can tell because of the way he acts around you."

"Really?"

"Yeah and you didn't even notice, did you? So, do you not like him that way?"

"It's not that I don't like him. I just don't really know. I don't think I've let myself like him in that way. My friends don't really think I should hang out with him, and so I tell myself over and over that he's my boss and it's better that we are just friends. I don't want a relationship to get in the way of work. I love my job, and if we didn't work, I would have to quit."

"Maybe. But he's not a jerk like that. You wouldn't have to just quit. I think he would let you do what you wanted or let you figure something out. But honestly Kelly, I don't think that you should let that get in the way of how you feel. It's just a job after all. Also, stop listening to your girlfriends. They mean well, but they are not always right."

"You know, I've never thought about it that way. I haven't let myself give it a chance. Not that I've really had a chance until today. For the last few months, I've listened to everyone else telling me how wrong it would be to get too involved with Vin. I wondered for months if he liked Natalie when instead, he maybe liked me? James, I feel so upset. I handled today so wrong. What's worse is that I don't even know how to fix it."

"You thought he liked Natalie? No. I mean he likes her as a friend, but that's it. Kelly, you can fix this, you just need to tell him why you acted the way you did today and figure out how you really feel about him and then tell him."

While I'm home for Thanksgiving, I tell Mum everything about Vin, and what my friends have told me to do about the situation. She tells me to stop worrying about everyone else and just go with my heart. Basically, everything that James said.

My Mum and I made plans for her to spend the following weekend with me in the city. She suffers from multiple sclerosis. This disease often makes it difficult for her to get around. We can't do all the things we love to do together. However, she has been feeling well enough the last few weeks. Mum wants to do a little shopping and have some girl time. Next weekend is the beginning of December and Christmas in Chicago will be in full swing. I'm thrilled.

Thanksgiving weekend comes and goes. I don't see Vin when I come back to the city. I don't know why I didn't text him. I feel really shy to see him, and I don't know how to start the conversation. I need to figure out how I'm really feeling. At work the following week, things are definitely not the same. We are both friendly to each other and still work on projects together, but we act like we are too busy to talk.

I pick Mum up from the train Friday evening and take a cab to my apartment. I'm so excited to spend this time with her. It's going to be a great girls weekend. I can't believe she hasn't seen my new studio yet! I'm so excited as I open my front door.

"Darling! It looks so cozy in here. You have done such a wonderful job making it your home. Oh, look, little Gracie. How does she like it here?"

"She loves it, we both do. I absolutely love the location." I look out my front window. "You know it's been my dream to live so close to Michigan Avenue, and it's just a block away."

"Yes, it is, you have done well for yourself. Dad and I are really proud of you."

"Thank you, Mum." I walk over and give her a giant hug.

We spend the evening cozied up in my studio, watching TV, eating chips and salsa, and drinking wine. It's nice to just spend quality time with my Mum.

In the morning, we get ready and head out to *Stan's Donuts*, my favorite donut place in the city. It is just off Michigan, and it has a cute café. We order a few donuts to share: the blueberry fritter, a Nutella pocket, the toffee cake, and two vanilla lattes.

"Do you like the donuts, Mum?"

"Yes, a bit rich for me, but they are very good."

"So, I know we can't do too much walking, but we can just go to a few stores that are right around here. Are you feeling okay to do that?"

'Yes, darling. I really want to go with you for a bit and start doing some Christmas shopping. I really want to get something nice for your Dad."

We end up shopping for a little over an hour, then decide to go to *Ghirardelli* to enjoy hot chocolate before we go back to my apartment. Mum can rest before dinner. We plan to have dinner at *Tavern on Rush* in the Gold Coast. I have never been there, but it looks good, plus it's another restaurant on my list. Even though the walk isn't too far from my apartment, we take a cab, so Mum doesn't have to walk in the cold.

The host seats us in the bar area next to the window. We chat about the twinkly holiday lights and how we love the way the streets are all decorated for the holidays. It's starting to feel like Christmas. We each order a glass of red wine and a bowl of tomato soup with a side of twice baked potatoes. A perfect meal on a chilly evening. I can't remember the last time that Mum and I have gone out for a meal together.

"This is so nice Mum. I'm glad we were able to do this, this weekend. I feel bad that I haven't come home as much the last few months. I've been so caught up with everything going on in the city."

"Well, you know I would love to see you more, but I understand that you're just trying to make a life for yourself here. Both Dad and I understand that. You have to do what you need to do to be happy. Speaking of what you need to do, have you talked to Vin lately? Have you sorted things out with him?"

"Well. No, not really. We have not really spoken much this week. I'm not sure how he is feeling now, what I should say, or how to start the conversation."

"Well, I definitely think you need to talk to him. He has after all been a good friend to you the last few months."

"Yeah, I know. He really has." I look over at my phone as it beeps and lights up with a text. "Oh my gosh! I can't believe this, but it's a text from Vin."

"Oh, really. Tell me, what did he say?"

"He asked, *How's hanging out with your Mom?*

"You have to respond to him. Go ahead and do it now."

"Okay." I look down at my phone and type back.

Good! We're having a lot of fun. It's really nice spending quality time together. She is going home tomorrow in the morning. How is your weekend?

I stare at my phone waiting for him to respond and my heart starts to beat a little faster.

"Well, what is he saying?"

"He hasn't responded yet." I put my phone back on the table, take a few sips of wine as we both stare at my phone. My phone beeps and lights up again. I reach over and grab it.

It's fine, nothing crazy. Is your Mum taking the train back in the morning?

Yes, she is. Why?

Well, maybe you should use my car. I know she has trouble getting around and it's a long train ride on Sundays, right? Might be a lot for her.

"He said that I should use his car to drive you home tomorrow, so you don't have to take the train."

"Awe, what a sweetheart."

"Well, do you want to do that instead?"

"Well, actually that would be nice. I am feeling a bit tired from the weekend."

"Okay. I'll tell him that we would love to use the car."

That would be so nice! Are you sure you don't mind?

Of course not. Just text me in the morning when you are coming by.

Okay, I will. Thank you so much, Vin.

No problem. See you in the morning.

Okay.

"Kelly, when you bring the car back to him, you really have to talk to him."

"I know Mum. I will."

I'm bummed the weekend is over already. We get into a cab and head over to Vin's apartment in the morning. He comes down to meet us and gives us both a hug.

"I've heard a lot about you, it's so nice to meet you, Vin."

"Same to you too. Did you have fun this weekend?"

"Yes, I did. It was lovely."

"What did you guys do?"

"We did some shopping, had some girl time at Kelly's apartment, and went out to dinner. Her place is really nice. She did well, it's so cozy. But, we should get going, so I can get home to your Dad. Once you bring Vin's car back, then maybe you two can hang out the rest of the day."

I give my Mum a smile. I know where she is going with this. "Okay, let's get going. Thank you again for the car. I will text you when I'm on my way back."

"Okay. Take your time."

We get in the car, and I turn to my Mum. "So, what do you think of him?"

"I think he's a sweet boy. If you want to date him, I think you should give it a go. You never know."

"Well, I'm not sure we'll actually date now after what happened. I'm still not sure what I want, but I definitely miss spending time with him, and we do need to talk."

Before I leave my parents' house, I have a quick coffee with Mum and Dad, and I text Vin that I will be in the city soon.

I drive into Marina City, and the valet guy takes his car. I text Vin, *I'm here.* He comes down a few minutes later.

"Hey. How was the traffic?"

"Not bad at all. Thanks for letting me drive your car to take my Mum home. It would have been a bit much for her to take the train."

"Oh yeah, of course."

"So, what are you doing the rest of the day. Do you have any plans?"

"No, not really. Nothing 'til later. I thought we could hang out this afternoon like your Mom said."

"Well, we can just grab a coffee and figure out something to do? My favorite holiday drink is the peppermint mocha at Starbucks. We could also walk around and maybe do some shopping?"

"Okay. But, didn't you shop yesterday with your Mum?"

"Yeah, but there are a few other places I would like to go."

"Okay, that's fine."

We walk together without saying much as we head toward the Starbucks. I'm really not sure how to start the conversation, and I don't think he knows what to say either. A part of me just wants to forget it, because we are hanging out now and everything seems somewhat normal. We grab our peppermint mochas and have fun browsing around some of the stores. We joke around in Nordstrom about some of the over-the-top holiday items, and that seems to break the ice between us a little more.

"Hey, I know a perfect holiday-ish thing we can do. It's something that's been on my list. Are you hungry? I haven't eaten much today."

"Yep, I would rather check out something new then shop. Where is it?"

"It's in the Gold Coast. It's the *Restoration Hardware*. It's a huge restored building, and the showroom has multiple floors."

"But, what about food. Can you eat there?"

"Yeah, there's a gorgeous café in the middle. At least it looks gorgeous from the Instagram photos."

We walk across the city to *Restoration Hardware* and the inside looks like a mansion. We put in my name for the café. It's a forty-five-minute wait, so we spend time exploring each floor.

Each room is decorated with beautiful RH furniture and accessories. I have my eye on a few things, including one of the faux fur blankets. My phone buzzes and I have a text that our table is ready. We head back downstairs toward the café, and we are seated on one of the couches in the middle of the room. The roof is another atrium. It really is so pretty in here with the garden-style tables and couches and a water fountain in the middle of the room. We order afternoon tea and share a cheese board, and a burger. I take a few photos for my blog before we start eating.

"What are you doing this evening?"

"Well, actually my parents are here."

"They are? From New York?"

"Yeah, just for a few days. My Mom wants to go to dinner tonight and afterward go to *Zoo Lights*. She loves going every year."

"That sounds fun. I haven't been to *Zoo Lights* yet."

"Do you want to come to dinner with us and go."

"Meet your parents and go to dinner?"

"Yeah."

"Hmm. I'm not sure. Maybe you should just hang with them and then if it's not too late, maybe we can watch a holiday movie after. Have you ever seen *Love Actually*? It's my favorite holiday movie. I have to watch it every year."

"Okay. Yeah. If it's not too late, I can come over after and watch it with you."

Around eight-thirty, there's a light knock at my door. I open the door, I give Vin a big smile when I see him standing there.

"Hey! I'm glad you decided to come over. How was hanging out with your parents."

"It was good."

"You still okay to watch the movie? If we start it now. It won't end too late."

"It's your favorite holiday movie, right?"

"Yep, it is.

"Okay, then, let's watch it."

TWENTY-SIX

"So, what did you think of the movie?"

"I liked it, I can see why you like it so much."

"Yep, it's the best, and it always gets me so excited for Christmas. I haven't done anything extra holiday-ish yet in the city. I've only really seen the holiday lights and the decorations around Michigan Avenue and maybe a few holiday drinks."

"Okay, well after work this week we can go to the *Christkindlmarket*. My Mom loves going there too whenever she's here. We can get some mulled wine and German food."

"Okay, yeah let's do that. There's also something else on my list that I read about. An old theatre in Southport called *Music Box Theatre* is playing *It's A Wonderful Life* during the holidays. I think it would be cool see that movie in an old theatre. They have showings on Saturday afternoons, and since we like movies, maybe we can go? What do you think?"

"I've never seen *It's a Wonderful Life*."

"You haven't?"

"No."

"Okay, then." I reach over and grab my laptop. "I think you will love it, let me see if I can get tickets for next Saturday."

As we walk into the *Music Box Theatre*, I already know this is the perfect thing to do to get us into the holiday spirit. The theatre is charming, decorated with traditional Christmas decorations. We get in the concession line and order hot spiced wine, popcorn, and my favorite movie candy, Sno-Caps. We walk toward our seats. Someone dressed as an elf is playing Christmas songs on the piano. A few minutes later carolers come out, and everyone joins in a sing-a-long. The movie begins, and I'm excited to watch the movie in the old theatre as it was meant to be seen, and for Vin to see it. Every time Mr. Potter comes on the screen, people in the theatre start to hiss and then cheer for George Bailey throughout the movie. I always get a little teary-eyed at the end of the movie, and we stay in our seats for a few minutes after it's over.

"Wow, it was so amazing to see that movie in this theatre. I loved all the caroling before the movie. That was really so much fun."

"I thought it was great. I'm glad we did this. It was way better than I thought."

"I'm glad we did this too. Thank you for going with me." Before I know what I'm doing, I reach over to grab his hand as we follow the crowd out of the theatre.

It's the last Friday before Christmas. We are playing Christmas music in the office, and I plan on ordering lunch today for everyone. I also brought in some holiday cookies and candy canes to make the office feel a little more festive. We are all excited that it's not only Friday but also that we have a long week off work.

James, Jillian, and even Kourtney said they all want to go to *SoPo* for some drinks and dancing tonight. I'm totally down for that. Since James and I have talked about this place so much over the last few months, I think Jillian and Kourtney are excited to see what is so great about this bar. They both come over to my apartment, so we can all get ready together and take a cab north to meet up with James.

"You guys, I don't want you to think this is somewhere really fancy. I don't want you to be disappointed when you walk in. It's just a fun spot, and the DJ plays really fun music, and if you like martinis, they have tons to choose from, all for five dollars, all night long."

"Well, I like music and martinis, and I'm excited to go."

Kourtney looks out the window and checks something on her phone. "You guys, it's really starting to snow. Maybe we should just order some food and stay here."

"No, let's go. Kelly has been telling us about this place for so long. We will only go out for a little bit."

It ends up taking us thirty-five minutes to get all the way up north to *SoPo*. We walk in, and James is at the bar with some guy. "What took you guys so long? Luckily, I found someone I knew so I wasn't sitting here all by myself."

"I'm so sorry! It's like a blizzard out there!"

"Really?"

"Yeah, it just started to really come down. I don't think we should make it too late of a night because it's going to be tough getting home."

"Okay. Agreed. But for now, let's get some drinks."

We find a bigger table toward the back and pile all our coats onto one of the chairs. We end up doing more sitting and drinking than dancing this evening. No one else is back here, so it feels like we have our own private little area. The main room with the bar isn't that busy at all. The snow must have stopped most people from coming out, which is rare for Chicago. Usually, the snow doesn't stop Chicagoans, and the bars are packed on Friday nights. I notice that James is busy texting on his phone. He keeps looking toward the front door and then looking back at his phone.

"Is someone else coming?"

"Maybe. But the weather is getting pretty bad outside."

"Well, we really shouldn't be out too much longer anyway. We should call it a night soon."

"We will. I just have to see if they are coming."

"Who?"

"Just a friend."

I give him a look. He is acting so strange. I'm pretty sure he is waiting for a guy he likes to show up. James looks at his phone again and looks up at the group.

"Okay. He's here."

"Who's here?" I look up toward the door just as Vin and his friend Vince walks in.

"Oh my gosh! What are you doing here!" I jump off my stool and rush over to him. I can't help myself, and I give him a huge hug, and he hugs me back.

"I just wanted to come and hang out with you guys."

"But it's terrible outside! I can't believe you came all the way up here. You are crazy."

"You're telling me. I had no idea Vin was going to drag me all the way up here. I don't even know where we are."

"I'm so sorry Vince. Well, you guys definitely need to get a drink."

"Okay. We will be right back." The two of them head to the bar, and James grabs two more seats to add to our table.

"James! I can't believe he came all the way up here."

"Seriously." Kourtney looks at me and then at James. "So, what's really going on with you two?"

"Honesty, nothing. We are just good friends." I look over at James, and he is sitting at the table just grinning.

"James! Tell me. Is that really true?"

"They are not dating. He likes Kelly though. I know that he does."

"How do you know that?"

"He told me th . . ."

"James stop! Kourtney, he told me a few weeks ago that he did have feelings for me, but not anymore. We haven't talked about it since."

"But I know he still does."

"Okay. James. Stop. Be quiet. They are coming back over."

The boys join us at our table, and I don't want to make it seem like we are talking about him.

"Okay, James. So, what are your plans for the holidays?"

He gives me a weird look. "What, oh, yeah. Umm, I'm just going home for a few days."

Finally, the bar starts playing some good songs, and we can't help but all get up and start dancing. James and I are dancing like we always do. Kourtney and Jillian are right along with us, and Vin and Vince are hanging back a bit watching the rest of us. We get another round of drinks and keep on dancing. Vin and Vince finally join in and, I think at this point, all of us have forgotten that there's a blizzard outside. James whispers to me that he will be right back and suddenly Vin and I are left alone to dance.

"What made you come all the way up here?"

"I wanted to come hang out with you before you went home for a few days."

"I'm not leaving 'til Tuesday."

"So, I like hanging out with you. I told you that."

"I know. Me too." As we are dancing, I notice that we are moving away from the group.

"Remember that thing I told you a few weeks ago?"

"Vin, I'm so sorry, I handled it so wrong. I was so rude."

"It's okay. I get it. I'm your boss. It was awkward for you. I don't want to make you feel weird."

"You don't make me feel weird."

"Okay. Well, that's good."

I look up at him, and I feel his lips on mine. I kiss him back, but for just for second because I quickly remember where I am. I'm sure all our friends are now watching us. I quickly pull away.

"Sorry. Wasn't that okay?"

I respond by giving him another kiss.

On Sunday morning, I meet James early at this spot called *La Creperie* in Lakeview. James is heading back home in a few hours, and he wanted to meet for brunch before he leaves. *La Creperie* is very quaint and cozy. It has a tiny bar in the front, along with a fireplace, and a bigger room in the back. They also have a garden patio in the summer. James is sitting at the table right by the fire.

"Morning!"

"Okay. Sit down. Tell me everything that happened on Friday night."

"Nothing more happened than a kiss or two."

"So, are you guys like dating now?"

"No. We haven't really talked about it. It was just a kiss."

"Just a kiss? Umm, it's kind of a big deal. Do you like him?"

"I like him. Wow. That's the first time I have actually said that out loud."

"Yes! Thank gosh, you're finally admitting your feelings. So, date him! What's the problem?"

"No problem. It just hasn't happened yet."

The rest of the weekend I finish my Christmas shopping, clean my apartment, get everything ready for Gracie, and pack everything I need to take home for Christmas. I spend Monday watching Christmas movies and working a little on my blog. My phone beeps. There's a text from Vin. I haven't really talked to him much since Friday night.

Hey, do you have a lot of stuff to bring home?

Kinda.

Cool. I will pick you up tomorrow and drive you to the train.

Are you sure?

Yep. I want to see you before you go home for Christmas. What time is your train?

10:35

Okay. I'll see you tomorrow.

In the morning, Vin drives me to Union Station. He parks in front of the station gets out of the car to help me with all my stuff.

"I'm sorry to do this to you, but I have another bag for you to bring home."

"Really? What is it?"

"It's a present for you."

"You didn't have to do that. Now I feel bad because I don't have anything for you."

"No, you didn't have to. I just wanted to get you a little something."

"Okay, well, thank you for driving me, and for the gift."

I give him a big hug, and we hold onto each other a little longer than usual. As I pull away, I notice he is holding onto my hand.

"Have a great Christmas."

"You too Kelly. I'm sure we will talk while you are home. I can pick you up from the station since you will probably have lots of bags."

"Okay, thanks, that would be great. I'll see you in a few days then."

A few hours later, I'm finally at home. Mum and I are baking our traditional English favorites for Christmas. This is one of my favorite things to do with my Mum during the holidays. *A Christmas Story* is playing in the background, and we are drinking wine as we bake sausage rolls and mince pies.

"So, guess what Mum."

"What darling?"

Vin got me a present. He gave it to me when he dropped me off at the train this morning."

"Really? What did he get you?"

"I don't know. I haven't opened it yet."

"Well, open it, you don't have to wait 'til Christmas."

"Okay, I'll go get it." I giggle and run out of the room. I grab the gift and run back to the kitchen. I place it on the kitchen table and start to unwrap the paper. I pull back the wrapping paper and stop.

"What's wrong? What is it?"

"If this is what I think it is, I'm going to freak out. I will feel so awkward if he has spent this much money on me."

"Okay, what is it?" I unwrap the rest of the box and show my Mum.

"Oh, Kelly. He didn't buy you one of those expensive purses."

"I don't know. Let's see." I nervously open the box and look inside.

It's not a bag. It's not a wallet. It's another box. I pick up the next box and open it. There's another small box.

"Why would he get you all boxes?"

"I don't know?"

I open the last box and inside is a gift card to Louis Vuitton. I show my Mum.

"Do you think he gave you a gift card, so you get the bag you want?"

"I hope not. We're not even dating, and that is such a major gift to give someone." I open the sealed card and see it's a gift card for twenty-five dollars along with a note.

Kelly,

Merry Christmas. When you finally save up enough money to get your bag, you can use this $25 to pay the tax.

Vin

I start cracking up, and I immediately grab my phone to call Vin. "I can't believe you did that! You totally freaked me out."

I just hear him laughing on the other end of the phone. "I thought that would surprise you. I know I gotcha good! Did you really think I would buy you something that expensive? I don't even know what's going on with us."

"You sure are a funny guy! I honestly wasn't sure. It would have been a bit much."

"When we went into Louis Vuitton a few weeks ago, you told me how much you love the history of the brand, you knew about all the bags, and that the Speedy 30 is your favorite. So then, I went back and told the guy at Louis Vuitton what I wanted to do, he thought it was funny and went along with it."

"Well, thank you so much for the gift card. I can honestly say, you really did get me!"

TWENTY-SEVEN

NEW YEAR'S EVE...

"So, are you coming with us tonight?"

"Yeah, I guess so."

"Wait, do you not want to?"

"I do Kourtney. I am sorry. I'm just . . . never mind. I'm coming for sure, it will be fun."

I head back to my desk and sit down. I'm feeling a little bummed. I have talked to Vin pretty much every day since he gave me that crazy gift for Christmas, but he hasn't mentioned anything about New Years to me. We still aren't dating. We still haven't really even talked about anything that's going on with us. However, I just figured that maybe he would ask me to do something or at least ask what I'm doing for New Years.

I wait all day and nothing. He has had plenty of time to ask me, and we have talked all day long. Maybe he has just forgotten that it's New Years? It's possible. Feeling crappy I walk over to James desk.

"Hey. Vin hasn't asked me at all about New Years. What should I do? I feel a little bummed about it."

James looks up at me and sighs. "Well, you could ask him, Kelly. Why does it have to be the guy all the time with you girls? It's not really fair."

"I didn't even think of that. I was too busy thinking he should ask me. Ugh, well, it's too late now. I already made plans with Kourtney. She invited me to a house party since I didn't have any plans. I didn't want to sit home by myself."

"Well, that's kind of dumb. I'm sure you wouldn't have been alone. I doubt Vin would let you be alone."

"James, you are so right! I'm so stupid! Why do I keep messing up like this? He is going to be so mad at me again. Now, I have no idea what I should do? I feel like such an idiot."

"Yep, this time you really are."

I roll my eyes at James. "Thanks for the support."

"Hey, this is all you, not me."

I take a deep breath and go back to my desk. I sit at my desk 'til after five. I wish everyone as they leave a Happy New Year. Kourtney walks out and tells me she will text me the address. About ten minutes after five, Vin comes by with his coat on, ready to leave for the day.

"Hey, you ready?"

"Ready for what?"

"Well, I figured we could go to dinner and just hang out. See where the night takes us."

I am such an idiot. I grab my things and follow him out the door.

"Where do you want to eat? I'm sure there's a new place you have wanted to try."

"Vin, I can't go with you."

"Why not? What happened?"

"Nothing happened. I just . . . I made plans for tonight. You didn't ask me to do anything, so I just figured you were doing something else."

"Why would you think that? We have been hanging out all the time the last few weeks." He looks really hurt.

"I'm so sorry. I feel terrible. I should have asked, but you didn't ask me either."

"I didn't think I had to. I just thought it was a given."

We walk out together onto Michigan Avenue like we have done

so many times before. The street is busy as usual, there are light flurries in the air, and it's getting cold. I wrap my coat tighter around me.

"So, where are you going tonight?"

"Kourtney asked me to go to a house party."

"Oh, and so you can't cancel?"

"I would feel bad if I did."

"So, that's it. You are going to go?"

"I feel like I have to."

"Okay, have fun then." He turns and walks away.

"Vin! Vin! Please! Don't go!"

I try calling out to him over and over. He turns the corner, and he's gone. I feel like I could cry. I feel sick. Why did I tell Kourtney I would go with her? I have made such a huge mistake. Again. When she asked me if I wanted to go with her and her fiancé, I knew in my gut it was wrong. Right now, I would rather have no plans than go to this party.

I get on the bus to take the short ride home. I wished right now that I was heading to dinner with Vin. Once I'm home, I call Kourtney.

"Just come! You can see him tomorrow. The party will be fun! It's really dumb if he's mad at you. It's not like you guys are a couple. So, you kissed. You have always said you are just friends."

She just didn't understand "Okay, I'll be there."

"You better! See you soon!"

I try calling Vin. No answer. I slowly get ready and leave for the party. The cab ride takes forever. It is all the way over in Wicker Park and it is New Year's Eve. Once I get to the party, I see Kourtney and her fiancé, and they both wave me over. I put on a smile and head over. Kourtney is trying to introduce me to all of her fiancé friends, but I just don't care. I don't want to be rude to them, but I just can't stop thinking about Vin and what happened after work.

I check my phone over and over. Nothing from Vin. I sent him a text on the way over in the cab, but he hasn't responded. It's only nine-forty, and I have a long time 'til midnight. I hang out with

Kourtney. She and her fiancé are having fun with their friends. I sip on my drink and stand there, just watching everyone around me. Kourtney is clearly a little annoyed with me, but at this point, I don't care. I keep checking my phone. Nothing. He must have decided to go out with his friends.

Finally. It's almost midnight. The music is turned down, and the TV is on. Everyone is partying in New York at Times Square. It had just turned midnight an hour before on the East Coast. Some guy turns the TV onto WGN so we can watch the Chicago version of the countdown. Now, we have three minutes to go. The cameras go back and forth to a variety of different hotel parties that are going on throughout the city. One minute to go. I just wished that this night would have gone so much differently.

The countdown starts: 10! . . . 9! . . .8! . . . 7! . . . 6! . . . 5! . . . 4! . . . 3! . . . 2! . . . 1!

Everyone shouts, "Happy New Year!" There's cheering and whistles blowing and horns honking.

Kourtney grabs me and squeezes me in a tight hug. "Happy New Year!"

I hug her back. "Happy New Year! Listen, don't be mad but I have to go."

"What! You're leaving now? You will never get a cab right now."

"I'm sorry. I just have to go."

"Okay, if you really have to go. Be safe! Text me tomorrow."

"Okay, will do."

I run out of the house as fast as I can and onto the street. It's snowing like crazy, but I don't care. I pull out my phone and call Vin. His phone rings and rings and he finally answers.

"Hello. Kelly?"

"Are you there? Where are you?"

"My friends dragged me out. Hold on a second. I can't hear you."

I'm freezing in my dress and coat, standing out in the cold, but I hang on. I'm not going to mess up again. A minute goes by, and I hear his voice again. He also sounds like he is outside.

"Hello?"

"Vin, I'm so, so sorry! I messed up really bad again. I feel awful. Tonight has been terrible. I just thought about you the whole night. I just wish I would have done things so differently. All night, I just kept thinking about how I wished I had gone to dinner with you."

Tears start forming, and I'm trying to hold back from crying. "Can you forgive me? I'm so sorry! I just want to be with you. Only you."

"It's okay. I should have asked you, but I figured we would be spending New Year's together. I just want to spend all my time with you."

"I know. Me too. I should have asked you too."

"Kelly, since I'm your boss, I never wanted to push you. I always just left things in your court."

"I know. I should have figured that out sooner."

"Are you outside?"

"Yeah, it's freezing!"

"I'm standing outside too. I'm going to try and get a cab and call you back. You do the same."

"Okay."

I try for over twenty minutes to get a cab. I keep running back into the house to stay warm and then try again. This is the worst night ever. I see some girls getting in a cab, and I run over to them.

"Hey, where are you guys going?"

"We are going downtown."

"Oh, can I please get in? I really need to get downtown. Anywhere closer to home would be great. I've been trying to get a cab for ages."

"Okay, yeah get in, it's freezing outside."

"Thank you so much."

I squeeze into the backseat. I text Vin that I finally got in a cab.

Me too. I thought maybe we could meet up, but it's awful out so just head home. I will call you as soon as I get home.

I'm so bummed that we are not meeting up, but I totally understand. It's late, everywhere is crazy, and it's a snowy mess outside.

Okay, talk soon.

Just as I walk into my apartment, my phone is ringing. I answer and run over to my bed and get under my covers to keep warm.

"Hello?"

"Hey."

"Getting home was terrible."

"It was and this whole night was terrible. My friends came over and dragged me out. I was just going to chill at home on the couch."

"Vin, I'm so sorry. I really hope you can forgive me."

"I can forgive you. Well, we should maybe get some sleep. It's getting late. But first, what are you doing tomorrow?"

"Something with you, I hope. Let's have a Kelly and Vin in the city kind of day. Maybe we could try the deep-dish pizza at *Pequod's Pizza?*"

"Okay. I'll pick you up tomorrow."

"Okay. Goodnight."

"Goodnight."

"Hey, by the way, Happy New Year."

"Happy New Year to you too."

I lay back in my bed feeling warm, cozy, and extremely happy. I think about all the things I have experienced this year, lots of ups and downs, my job, and friends I have made. It's been quite a year. I think back to all those times I was watching *The Office,* wondering if I would ever meet my Jim?

Well, I did. I have met my own Jim, and he was right there in my office all along.

A GIRL'S GUIDE TO CHICAGO CHECKLIST

During my first year in Chicago, city life was so new to me, and I had so much fun exploring all the sights, restaurants, and the bar scene. Most of the places that I visited during my first year have become an important part of my life, filled with special memories, and they are still my favorite places to go with my husband, friends, and family.

Use this checklist to help you explore Chicago. These are my personal hotspots, and all are mentioned in my book. They can be your own girl's guide to explore some of my favorite places in the amazing city of Chicago. I hope you enjoy them as much as I do.

☐ Marshall Field's/Macy's on State Street
111 N. State Street *(This is the first store I visited as a little girl during my first trip to Chicago. Visit during the holidays, it is magical, and dining at the Walnut room is a must.)*

☐ Michigan Avenue
The Magnificent Mile *(Aptly named, this street will never get old for me for all the shopping, dining, enjoying a stroll, and even people watching.)*

☐ Lake Michigan

The Lakefront *(There is nothing better than walking, biking, or jogging along the lake trail. There are miles of beaches, parks, gardens, and it is the perfect place to spend a day enjoying the sunshine.)*

☐ Osteria Via Stato

620 N. State Street *(You can enjoy their amazing Italian tapas and the fresh bread with fresh garlic and oil is the best.)*

☐ Grand Lux Cafe

600 N. Michigan Avenue *(This is great for a quick, easy lunch. It is more of a tourist spot.)*

☐ SoPo

(SoPo sadly closed. This bar holds fond memories for me. I just had to include it.)

☐ Gold Coast

Rush and Oak Street *(A beautiful neighborhood for shopping and fine dining anytime of the year. The Gold Coast is a luxury neighborhood that also features many designer shops.)*

☐ Freds Chicago at Barneys

15 E. Oak Street *(Perfect for a fancy 'ladies who lunch' kind of spot.)*

☐ Lao Sze Chuan

520 N. Michigan Avenue *(Best Chinese in Chicago. You have to order the Tony's Chicken, Crispy Shrimp w/ Lemon Sauce, and the crab rangoon.)*

☐ POPS for Champagne

601 N. State Street *(Cute downtown wine bar. They offer a world-class selection of champagne and full-service bar. Perfect place for an after-work cocktail or host a special event.)*

☐ **Green Street Meats**
112 N. Green Street *(Known for its BBQ, pulled pork, brisket, and more. The West Loop is full of amazing fun restaurants like this one.)*

☐ **United Center**
1901 W. Madison Street *(This is not only the home of the Chicago Bulls and Blackhawks, but it is also the place to see major artists in concerts.)*

☐ **Underground**
56 W. Illinois Street *(A popular nightclub in Chicago, once named "One of the Sexiest Places in the World". It is a trendy nightclub that hosts special entertainment events and features popular DJs.)*

☐ **Angelina Ristorante**
3561 N. Broadway Street *(This is a authentic, cozy, Italian gem in Lakeview.)*

☐ **J9 Wine Bar**
1961 N. Halsted Street *(In the heart of Lincoln Park, this bar offers a wide selection of fine wine, cocktails, cheese and charcuterie platters in a cozy at-home atmosphere.)*

☐ **Mercadito**
108 W. Kinzie Street *(In the heart of River North, it offers authentic Mexican cuisine, signature tacos, and the best margaritas in the city. You must ask for the regular margarita and add the spicy salt.)*

☐ *Cafe Ba-Ba-Reeba!*
2024 N. Halsted Street *(Authentic Spanish tapas and a variety of sangrias in Lincoln Park, a perfect place for a girls' night.)*

☐ **Ann Sather**
909 W. Belmont Avenue *(Offers breakfast and lunch menus, and the cinnamon rolls are a must!)*

☐ **Beatrix River North**
519 N. Clark Street *(One of the best brunch/lunch places. I love the egg white omelet. Ask for the brown sugar bacon and extra avocado. The almond chocolate croissants are amazing and, for lunch, I love the Straight A Salad.)*

☐ **Le Colonial**
937 N. Rush Street *(In heart of the Gold Coast, it's Chicago's famed Vietnamese restaurant beautifully styled in the era of the French Colonial Southeast Asia of the 1920s. It has the best lychee martini in the city, but you can't go wrong with anything on the menu.)*

☐ **Intelligentsia Coffee**
3123 N. Broadway Street *(Local favorite coffee bar that offers a variety of coffee, tea, and espresso. I love the vanilla latte.)*

☐ **Mortar and Pestle**
3108 N. Broadway Street *(Offers globally inspired cuisine and is a favorite neighborhood brunch spot. The homemade biscuits and homemade jam are the best.)*

☐ **Wrigley Field**
1060 W. Addison Street *(In Wrigleyville, it's the Home of the Chicago Cubs. This stadium is magical with its iconic ivy-covered outfield wall and hand-turned scoreboard. You have to see a baseball game. Don't forget your Chicago-style hotdog.)*

☐ **Parson's Chicken & Fish**
2952 W. Armitage Avenue *(casually served fried chicken and fish. Amazing backyard-style patio. This is a perfect place to sip on a famous Negroni slushy during the summer.)*

☐ **Cesar's Killer Margaritas**
2924 N. Broadway Street *(The name says it all. Favorite for authentic Mexican restaurant and giant margaritas.)*

☐ RPM Italian

52 W. Illinois Street *(Trendy, hot spot that offers freshly made pasta and great Italian tapas. Also, if you are a fan of the celebrity couple Giuliana and Bill Rancic, you will love this place. They are partners in this restaurant.)*

☐ John Hancock Building

875 N. Michigan Avenue *(Loved living so close to one of my favorite buildings. You have to enjoy a Godiva martini at the Signature Lounge, of course, by the windows. Also, the women's bathroom is the best in the city, when you go you will see why. The 360 Chicago observatory has the best view of Chicago.)*

☐ Drumbar at the Raffaello Hotel

201 E. Delaware Place *(Favorite fun speakeasy-style rooftop bar with great cocktails.)*

☐ Coq d'Or at The Drake Hotel

140 E. Walton Place *(The Drake Hotel is one of my favorite hotels. Built in 1933 after the repeal of prohibition, it was the second Chicago establishment to obtain a liquor license. Have cocktails at Coq d'Or and afternoon tea in Palm Court. It is a must-do in Chicago.)*

☐ The Peninsula Hotel

108 E. Superior Street *(The Bar is perfect for late-night cocktails. Enjoy the chocolate bar during the holidays in The Lobby. The garden in Shanghai Terrace is splendid for cocktails with friends or a special someone.)*

☐ Sunda

110 W. Illinois Street *(Asian cuisine. Fun and trendy sushi spot.)*

☐ Naoki Sushi

2300 N. Lincoln Park West *(A mix of classic and contemporary Japanese cuisine in a speakeasy-style restaurant. It has amazing fresh sushi and its location is a true hidden gem tucked behind the kitchen inside the Belden-Stratford.)*

☐ The Violet Hour
1520 N. Damen Avenue *(A secret hidden speakeasy. If you can find the entrance, it is worth the amazing cocktails and ambience inside.)*

☐ Smoke Daddy
1804 W. Division Street *(Favorite BBQ spot in Wicker Park)*

☐ The Riverwalk
along The Chicago River *(One of the best places to hang out in the summer. Multiple great bars for drinks, including City Winery.)*

☐ The Hampton Social
353 W. Hubbard Street *(Fun nautical spot and the best place for rosé all day.)*

☐ Millennium Park/Jay Pritzker Pavilion
201 E. Randolph Street *(One of the most beautiful parks in the city. Attend a concert or a movie at the pavilion. This is a summer favorite.)*

☐ RL Restaurant
115 E. Chicago Avenue *(Perfect spot for lunch or dinner after a day of shopping on Michigan Avenue, especially during the holidays.)*

☐ Cindy's at Chicago Athletic Association Hotel
12 S. Michigan Avenue *(Panoramic rooftop view for dining and delicious cocktails.)*

☐ Summer House Santa Monica
1954 N. Halsted Street *(Located in Lincoln Park, it offers a warm feel of the West Coast with beach house décor and California wines. It is a favorite spot to go when you want it to feel like it is summer.)*

☐ Eataly Chicago
43 E. Ohio Street *(I love to go here for a late-night dessert. The offer fresh pasta, pizza, Italian hot chocolate, and wine tastings.)*

☐ Mastro's
520 N. Dearborn Street *(The best steakhouse restaurant. Get the lemon drop martini, filet Oscar-style, lobster mash, and save room for the butter cake.)*

☐ Bijan's Bistro
663 N. State Street *(Great late-night spot and, yes, the French onion soup is really good!)*

☐ The Art Institute of Chicago
111 S. Michigan Avenue *(One of my favorite museums in the city. You have to see the Thorne Miniature Rooms.)*

☐ Star of Siam
11. E. Illinois Street *(A little hidden gem downtown and my favorite Thai restaurant in the city.)*

☐ 676 Restaurant at The Omni Hotel
676 N. Michigan Avenue *(My own hidden gem overlooking Michigan Avenue. I love to sit by the window and look out over The Magnificent Mile.)*

☐ Stan's Donuts
multiple locations *(My favorite donut place. Enough said, you must try these donuts.)*

☐ Ghirardelli Chocolate
830 N. Michigan Avenue *(Even though it is a chain, the hot chocolate and sundaes are really the best.)*

☐ Tavern on Rush
1031 N. Rush Street *(An upscale contemporary steakhouse. I love dining in the bar area in the winter and dining on the patio during the summer.)*

☐ Restoration Hardware (RH) and 3 Arts Club Café
1300 N. Dearborn Street *(Perfect place for afternoon tea or drinks with the girls. The Café is a sight-to-behold with its glass atrium ceiling, potted trees, and a magnificent chandelier.)*

☐ ZooLights at Lincoln Park Zoo

2001 N. Clark Street *(Zoo Lights is a popular holiday thing to do in Chicago. During the Christmas season, the Zoo is transformed by millions of lights and displays that make it look like a winter wonderland. Make sure you grab a hot chocolate first to keep you warm. The zoo is free and a wonderful place to visit any time of the year.)*

☐ Christkindlmarket

50 W. Washington Street *(It is one of the best and most beloved outdoor holiday markets inspired by German tradition in the Chicago Loop. Bundle up and sip on some delicious mulled wine.)*

☐ Music Box Theatre

3733 N. Southport Avenue *(This is a movie venue for independent and foreign films, cult, and classic films. If you are here during the Christmas holidays, you must see "It's a Wonderful Life." It is a tradition that I love to do every year.)*

☐ La Creperie

2845 N. Clark Street *(I love this little neighborhood gem for crepes, wine, or coffee. The back-garden patio is a favorite of mine during the summer.)*

☐ Pequod's Pizza

2207 N. Clybourn Avenue *(A local favorite for Chicago deep dish pizza.)*

If you are looking for more things to do in Chicago, *girlsguidechicago.com* has tons of guides for girls who love to have fun and want to explore some of the best places in the city.

While you use this checklist to visit these my favorite places, send photos of you with your girlfriends using the hashtag **#GGCBook**.

CPSIA information can be obtained
at www.ICGtesting.com
Printed in the USA
LVHW081954190519
618384LV00017B/792/P